ABOUT ST LEONARD'S

by Mike Umbers

Mostly Re-printed from
St Leonard's Parish Review
(1999-2015)

Edited by Lindsay Fairgrieve

Penumbra

*The lines are fallen unto us in pleasant places;
yea, we have a goodly heritage* - **Ps 16**

Copyright © Mike Umbers
All rights reserved *2015*

ABOUT ST LEONARD'S

by Mike Umbers

Mostly Re-printed from
St Leonard's Parish Review
(1999-2015)

Edited by Lindsay Fairgrieve

Front Cover and Frontispiece by Janine Umbers

Thanks to Artwrite Hythe Ltd., John Gabris
and Sean McNally for help with illustrations

ISBN 978-1-326-47182-8
Published by AudioArcadia.com

This book, which includes text and cover artwork, is sold on the
condition that it is not lent, resold, hired out, performed, recorded,
distributed, circulated or handed out by any other method in whatever
format to any other party, including third parties, agents, retailers or any
other source of distribution without the prior consent of the publisher. The
publisher can be contacted by email at info@audioarcadia.com

CONTENTS

Page No.

Hythe and its Church	7
The Slow Sure Growth of St Leonard's Church	10
The Street/Pearson Remodelling of St Leonard's	13
Faith in a Flat Pack	17
The Methodist Anglican Amalgamation	20
An Easter Sepulchre in the North Transept?	25
Not Forgotten	26
A Legacy of Love - and Self-Interest	28
Where Are We?	29
A 19th Century Battle: Church v Army	33
At War with Saltwood	36
Remembrance in Hythe	39
A War-Time Memory	43
Questions of Architecture	44
The Porch and Parvise	47
The Church's Former Reredos	51
A Green Man or a Gallic Gesture?	55
Ins and Outs of the Eagle	58
Science and the Bones	61
The Unanswered Riddle	65
Another Conundrum	69
Thoughts on Bones	73
A Re-think on the Crypt	77
An Exterior View	82
The Altar-ations of History	86
A Saxon Church in Hythe?	90
A Parish Treasure	94

An Architectural History	100
Tourist Trap	103
A Debate on Dates	108
Our Victorian Church	112
Turbulent Priests	116
An Historical Calendar	119

Note the family tombs below the terrace. The Deedes tomb is accessed from the South Transept (which the family re-built)

HYTHE AND ITS CHURCH

Many of these articles have been up-dated from articles which first appeared in the Parish Review. Others are newly written.

This book is my tribute to this amazing building and those who befriend it and worship in it. It is to be sold for the benefit of The Friends of St Leonard's.

This introduction was written at the request of Miss Flora Laundon for her 1991 Festival, 'A Time to Celebrate'.

If the citizens of Hythe built St Leonard's Church today, it wouldn't have a Tower, of course, (that would be an intrusion on the skyline), and it wouldn't have a Crypt (there's a Government ban on bones), the churchyard would be a car park, the pews would be replaced with stackable chairs to make room for the basketball pitch, and the Chancel would be a dual-purpose stage with electronic organ.

Those who did build it had rather different - and more durable - priorities: they intended it should reflect God's power and majesty: they spent money on quality materials, they filled it with colour to signify His glory; they lavished expertise on its design and craftmanship on its execution.

This town's first location was at West Hythe, where the Romans built their sheltered harbour: as that silted up, a new harbour was developed to the East, and the people migrated round it. It was busy with trading vessels and the activities of the fishermen. With each advance in prosperity, the Church was extended, improved, and beautified.

Until 1794, when the Town Hall was built, the Mayor, Jurats and Bailiffs met in the Parvise over the church porch; for two hundred and fifty years, in that small unheated candle-lit room, these worthies discussed the governance of Hythe, afterwards groping down the steep stone steps, chatting of a birth, a death, the price of a sheep, the death of a king, or the threat from France, and finally descending the dark streets and walkways back to their homes.

Never let us regard these people with contempt: superstitious they were and ignorant of science, but they had a spiritual way of thought as complex and sophisticated in its way as any modern philosophy - and for sure their gossip was no different from ours!

Nor did they live in a backwater. Think of any major historical event: the Plagues, the Reformation, the Spanish Armada, the French Wars, the German Wars - every one of these affected Hythe, and every one impinged in some way on St Leonard's Church and can be traced in its appearance or contents today.

Look merely on the graffiti: modern graffiti is deplorable, graffiti six hundred years old is history. Those touching crosses scratched in hope or thanksgiving or penitence; that ship - a prayer for a safe voyage or a full catch? These amateur doodles reflect the intimate relationship of medieval man with his God and witness a faith which is sure of God's interest in his concerns.

We would love to know more of this relationship. Did they meet in the Church to ask Him to take away the Plague? How did they react to the arrival of Cromwell's Puritans, charged with the joyful task of destroying works of art because they were papist images? The congregation and their forefathers had paid for these - now they were smashed, the altars gone, the familiar bright rich paintings covered in whitewash.

The impact on these ordinary people, the disorientation, are unimaginable. Yet, as in all human affairs, stability returns; the long reign of Elizabeth brought back order gradually. Then a new Prayer Book set forth the new way, with constant reference to continuity with the old, services to take place *'as it hath been in times past'*.

With the final loss of its harbour, Hythe sank into poverty. Its church reflected that as well: near derelict, with too few citizens to fund even its repair, still less its improvement. This phase, too, passes; a new energy of faith - condemned often nowadays because Victorian taste is not our taste - and a new prosperity repaired the roof and paid for refurbishment.

We inherit a church which reflects the phases of decorative fashion and charts the flow of history over a thousand years; give thanks for our inheritance, preserve it, enhance it and pray in it as so many like ourselves have done before us.

THE SLOW SURE GROWTH OF ST LEONARD'S CHURCH

This drawing appeared in the Builder Magazine of July 1855. The accompanying text tells the reader that: *'The Station at Westenhanger offers no great temptation to the traveller, but if he can make up his mind to leave the train there he will be rewarded with a pleasant walk ... and an opportunity of examining one of the best specimens of ecclesiastical architecture in the country'*. ['Saltwood for Hythe' Station was not built until 1873 so before that Westenhanger was the usual stop for Hythe]. Here was high praise indeed for St Leonard's Church, though how bare it looks to modern eyes!

Actually the author's praise is afterwards qualified: *'Internally the church has suffered greatly by modern and tasteless alterations. It would be impossible to say too much as to the ugliness of the ceilings, both in nave and chancel'*. This comment referred to the plaster ceilings which were hardly modern – they had been in place since the chancel was built. Fortunately they were removed in the dramatic renovations later in the 19th Century.

The 'en suite' sedilia and piscina shown in the other Builder Magazine drawing are integral to the design of the 13th Century chancel, and the 'string course' of incised rosettes and fleur de lys above the altar is *'better carved than similar work in Canterbury Cathedral'*, says our Church Guidebook – but we would say that. Probably the Archbishop sent his skilled masons down here at intervals, for

11

building works were proceeding in both places at the same time and Hythe was being given — I feel sure, deliberately — a design imitating on a smaller scale features of the Cathedral to impress the pilgrims en route in growing numbers to Saint Thomas à Becket's tomb.

A double sedilia is slightly unusual (though one, three and even four seaters exist). I have an irreverent vision of a tall thin gloomy priest and a short fat jolly one perching on the two seats during the long medieval Services. The special interest of the piscina is that it is a double one: there was only one short period of a few years when, by Papal decree, two bowls were needed.

Why did the Chancel have to wait over six hundred years to be completed at last by the Victorians? It is possible the Town simply ran out of money, or the death of Archbishop Stephen Langton in 1228 could have interrupted the work in which, as Lord of the Manor and resident in Saltwood Castle, he had taken a personal interest? Another suggestion is that there may have been some settlement of the stonework at the South-East corner, so it was thought wiser to pause before adding a mighty weight above.

The late Jack Barker, our Historian, speculated there could have been a blockade of the Channel Ports by the French, which cut off the supply of the Caen stone previously used and would account for the use of a rare Kentish rag and Purbeck marble for the columns, dark blue, full of fossils and polished.

A French blockade? There is something particularly modern in this explanation!

THE STREET/PEARSON REMODELLING OF ST LEONARD'S

From the 1830's onwards the Ecclesiologists wrought appalling damage on Parish Churches up and down the land as they gleefully destroyed the hated 'Prayer Book Churches' and set the clock back to pre-Reformation England in pursuit of the only acceptable Christian architectural style: 13th Century Gothic, as decreed by Pugin and the Camden Society.

Luckily for us, St Leonard's was already a medieval Gothic Church, cruciform in ground plan, with a Chancel, raised Sanctuary and Altar, forward-facing pews, off-set Pulpit, Eagle reading stand ... it needed only completion in detail and provision of vestments, candles and 'Hymns Ancient and Modern' to conform fully, and to achieve the approved 'dim religious glow'!

In the period 1875-87, JL Pearson, RA and GE Street, ARA - top Architects of the time (and Designers too, which would be thought unusual today) were brought in to complete the medieval vision for St Leonard's Church which had stalled in the 13th Century, probably as funds dried up or perhaps as Plague reduced the skilled work force.

Street (who had designed those famous Gothic Cathedral-like Law Courts in the Strand) was responsible for removing the plaster roof over the St Leonard's Nave (the previous lowering roof actually covered the little opening into the corridor over the Chancel Arch).

For the Nave and Aisles he chose red, black and cream floor tiles in a rather cosy domestic pattern to replace the stone slabs, giving a warmer effect, designed the marvellous marble Reredos showing the Deposition from the Cross (it was actually carved by Armstead, another top name at that time, and removed in 1936 to the South Choir Aisle), and he installed the bench pews and put in a new and lower pulpit. Actually his pulpit was thought rather dull in appearance and, later, glittering mosaic tiles were added, the donors paying eight pounds per panel.

Meanwhile Pearson, the all-rounder who designed the choir stalls, was also an expert in stone vaulting (exemplified in his designs for Truro Cathedral, and first practised here). He worked on the completion of the Chancel: the clerestory (the row of windows) high in the South wall of the Chancel was opened, and a similar clerestory and a triforium were created in the blank North wall, with rounded and pointed arches combined - a perfect fusion of styles, exactly like the 12th Century work in Canterbury Cathedral, albeit in sandstone, which you can still distinguish from the medieval Caen stone.

The six hundred and fifty year old wood and plaster 'temporary' roof was removed. In the centre and in the two choir Aisles was installed, *in stone,* to the great benefit of the acoustics, a vaulted roof to the medieval design. To be entirely accurate, we should say 'to what we must assume to be the medieval design', for the early master masons left no plans of their intentions.

The old printed Guide to the Church, by the late Jack Barker, describes how the technical problems were solved - with such success that only an expert can now see how it was done and how they had to fudge and bodge to make the ribs fit.

Where Pearson earned his fee was in determining the walls would take the additional weight without bowing outwards or sliding down the hillside, but an extra buttress against the South wall guarded against this eventuality.

During this Victorian period much of our stained glass was installed, but the final touch was the new East window. This, of course, did not survive the War. I will court controversy by giving my opinion that Wallace Wood's bright 1951 replacement window, bravely modern in this place, perfectly complements with its colour and joyfulness the grey formality of the remaining 13th *and* the 19th Century windows.

The Chancel is the glory of our Church; how amazing to think its design was conceived around the time of Magna Carta. It must surely have awed the pilgrims who were beginning to pour through Hythe Port en route to the tomb of Becket, murdered just thirty or forty years before.

If you look at today's Visitors' Book, the comments made over and over again are *'grand'*, *'peaceful and lovely'*. A German visitor even writes *'Toll'* - the equivalent of *'brill'* which suggests a youngster also appreciates it.

How was work on this scale funded? The Reredos was paid for separately by a former curate in memory of his wife, and the pulpit panels by individual donors, but for the rest of the money the answer is on the plaque on the column near the organ: ***'By the loving care and zeal of the Rev TG***

Hall MA, Vicar, at a total cost of £10,000. Raised by Voluntary Contributions'.

No Lottery Grant then? No. Nor was there in the Millennium Year, 2000, when two hundred and fifty thousand pounds was needed; the National Lottery Commissioners told us, 'Hythe is rich enough to find that for itself'!' And so it proved.

Graffiti on St Christopher Column.
'Off to War': A 'Hule' single-masted pre-1450 vessel with side-steering oar and forecastles for archers.

FAITH IN A FLAT PACK
'How amiable are thy tabernacles' - Psalm 84

The old tin Church of St Michael attracted much public attention (even from some who had never actually been inside it) when the decision was taken in 2010 to close it as a place of worship, especially as there was every likelihood it would be dismantled and replaced (inevitably) by a 'box of flats' too large and too high for the site.

A petition to 'Save the Tin Tabernacle' met with an enthusiastic response. Its scale, character and construction are just so right on its tiny triangular plot, its history reflects social change as well as Victorian industrialisation and evangelism, and it is perfectly sited to perform a useful function as a Community Hall.

The success of the campaign was not a foregone conclusion for there are many similar churches, as you can see from the website www.tintabernacles.co.uk. Ours has only the altar and pulpit remaining of its original furnishings and fittings, but with so much public pressure, it was successfully Listed 'Grade II' in 2011.

An unfortunate consequence of being listed is that it can make a building less attractive to a prospective purchaser and so much harder to sell; there was a possibility that it would simply sit there, FOR SALE, unused, and at risk of vandalism and decay. The happy news is that it *was* quickly sold, has been re-painted without and reconfigured within.

Today it is run by its new and public-spirited owners as a venue for many useful activities, to the great benefit of the town. Equally happy is the result of the joining of its former congregation with the Methodist congregation on the other side of the Canal. Their church is now re-designated **'St Michael's Methodist-Anglican Church Centre'**.

Corrugated iron does not normally have many supporters. Some of us have experienced corrugated iron buildings in army camps; they are called Nissen huts, ugly to look at and cold to sleep in.

Think again about tin churches. Shake off your prejudices, and admit our little mission church had style and a pleasing atmosphere. The site was given by the Watts family and the disposal plan made it necessary to check the terms of the gift: donated land may carry provisos, eg. *'No offensive trade, shop or day school, tavern or tea garden...and no betting waging or gaming carried on...no spirituous or fermented liquors shall be sold in or upon any part of the said land or in any buildings erected thereon'*. We wondered if a covenant on these lines would be uncovered to restrict its future use as a community hall; fortunately none was, or even an innocent raffle may have been banned.

Back in 1892/3 a Committee selected the off-the-shelf church from a trade catalogue and the bill was paid for by the Rev'd FT Scott, a former Vicar. It was built cheaply to serve the working classes who had moved South of the Canal as the town expanded in the late 19th Century and who, we have to admit, were a little afraid of the 'Big Church on the Hill' with its snobbery and family-owned pews. You were never quite sure where you could sit and even less sure of a warm welcome (how different today!)

Many similar churches were put up across the land as stopgaps, until a 'proper brick building' could be funded. In Hythe, there was probably no thought of this, although those present at the opening on 19th September 1893 might have been surprised to think it would still be standing in 2009.

These quick-builds were erected to match the Non-conformist momentum of the period, when the Church of England had been left behind by the social changes of the Industrial Revolution, a mobile population, and changing styles of worship. But this was an Anglican Church, dedicated by the Archdeacon of Maidstone.

The manufacturing revolution had produced the technology to match the need; a supplier could deliver a 30ft x 20ft chapel to the nearest Railway Goods Yard for seventy-seven pounds and ten shillings; a 60ft x 30ft one could be supplied and erected on your prepared site for one hundred and forty-five pounds, though the artisan congregation was often able to do much of the work. A little bell tower like ours was an extra.

From its earliest days, a Sunday School was in operation here. In the days of large families and few bedrooms, Sunday Schools gave mothers and fathers a brief period to themselves in an empty house, and children were packed off quickly after Sunday lunch. I do like the story that the children from the Army Married Quarters in Reachfields, who were sent to St Michael's, had to pass The Citadel. It turned out later that they had been waylaid and ambushed en route, whether by chance or design, by the Salvation Army Sunday School!

THE METHODIST ANGLICAN AMALGAMATION

In 2010/2011 Parish discussion was dominated by the decision to sell the 'Tin Tabernacle' and to amalgamate the congregations of St Michael's and the Methodist Church. I have summarised the events of that period from various articles in the Parish Review.

A friend tried to visit a London church recently - she couldn't get in because it was locked, but she read the notice outside:

ONE CHURCH, TWO CONGREGATIONS

We are not the first parish to realise the sense of combining into fewer buildings. But the difference here is that we are to be:

ONE CHURCH, ONE CONGREGATION

The opening Service in the St Michael's Methodist Anglican Centre on 2nd October 2011 marked a new beginning, an *amalgamation* of the present Methodist and Anglican congregations (a mere fifteen years after that famous Commitment to Mission and Unity was jointly signed by the Anglican and Methodist hierarchies). There was much administrative and financial detail to be decided and legally set out - even the name of the shared church: it became **St Michael's Methodist Anglican Church Centre**.

The first decision (an easy one) was that the Centre would be in the former Methodist Church - a brick building with a fine organ and additional rooms and facilities - and the corrugated iron Chapel would be sold.

Both sides had to give a little: Sunday Services at 11.00 a.m. (a little earlier for one group, a little later for the other), with consequent disruption of our established domestic patterns; a traditional Methodist Sunday Service on the fourth Sunday of the month, an Anglican Matins with a Book of Common Prayer Communion on the second Sunday, and Joint Services on the first and third Sundays.

It sounds so easy, but feelings came into it as well as practicalities. Old buildings tell the story of the people who built them and lived in them or, in this case, worshipped in them, and the Tin Church had earned much affection. For over a hundred years it had provided religious services, especially for Hythe's growing artisan population in the expanding area South of the Royal Military Canal, a population for whom St Leonard's Church on the hillside was distant and inconvenient of access, and even socially unwelcoming.

The Vicar of the day cherished an idea of building a more suitable and convenient place of worship for those who were unable or unwilling to attend St Leonard's. This was made possible by two generous gifts: an offer to pay for the building by a former Vicar, the Reverend FT Scott, and the provision of a site by the Watts family - a perfectly located triangle of land at the junction of Stade Street and Portland Road and adjacent to the Town Bridge.

In 1893 matters moved swiftly. An appeal for funds met with a generous response. The parts were ordered, delivered and assembled within a few months. It was intended to seat about two hundred and eighty people. It appeared in scale with its tiny site, and had a pretty bell-tower (an extra on the bill), pointed windows and door and, inside, painted wooden cladding.

A Mr Andrews gave an altar made from oak grown on his own land. This, and a neat oak pulpit, remained in use until the end of the building's life as a church.

Subscribers bought a two-manual organ (later replaced with a better one), lighting was by gas, and heating by coke stove.

The opening ceremonies took place on Tuesday, 19th September 1893 when the Archdeacon of Maidstone dedicated the building to St Michael and All Angels. In the course of time, the original wooden pews were replaced with comfortable chairs. Electric lighting and gas heaters were installed, as was the fitted carpet and, behind the scenes, a kitchen and lavatory.

The little church was also in frequent use as a venue for secular events such as talks and meetings; indeed it became almost a second 'church hall' within the parish, (with rather better parking than the mother Church or the Canon Newman Hall!) The building, though not pretentious, was both homely and dignified, inspiring real affection from its loyal congregation; its centenary was celebrated in 1993 with special services, a flower festival and tea parties.

'God is working his purpose out...' (New English Hymnal No 495)

The Last Service in the Tin Church took place on 25th September 2011 when a packed congregation from four Hythe churches brought in Harvest Home. Actually it was not so much an ecumenical service as a full Anglican Mass.

The Rev'd Desmond Sampson - in recent times the regular officiating clergyman there, though long retired - preached: *'I had a dream...'*, he told us (echo there of a rather famous speech from long ago in another country), but he didn't linger on the past. (We might have forgiven him for doing so, for he spoke from the pulpit he first climbed as a curate over forty-five years ago). Rather, he looked forward: his dream was of a rail journey; of reaching not a terminus but a junction; of crossing a river (for river, think Royal Military Canal), with a welcome awaiting us on the other side and a new future. Many others have been using metaphors like this recently, about this move: they can say what they like, but I cried.

Throughout the summer both the merging congregations have felt unsettled, ours more so as we are changing locations; of course, that shouldn't matter - the church is not buildings - but we are leaving our familiar home with all its memories of friends departed.

You have to tell yourself it is (as in the serenely optimistic Hymn 495) a step forward in a master plan, but God's railway timetable and route-planning have seemed even more opaque than usual recently. Whatever our hopes for the new Church Centre, we are witnessing the end of an era and the break-up of a fellowship. As we looked along the rows of chairs that day, some of us were seeing in our mind's eye the faces of departed friends in their old places.

The end-time actually came one week later, on 2nd October 2011, when a small group of the former congregation met in the echoing space to hear

Bishop Richard Llewellin and then the Vicar and Norman Woods too, thanking God for the little Church and its one hundred and eighteen year mission to Hythe.

Afterwards, we followed the Processional Cross over the Town Bridge, carrying the Silver Cross, the Bible, and the Communion Cup and Paten to their appointed places on the new 'made-to-measure' altar table in NEW St Michael's. And there, in the presence of Bishop Richard, the Town Mayor, the Vicar and Minister, and the 'management' of both churches, began the Inaugural Joint Service: there was a part for everyone, carefully crafted prayers were said, even the sermon was a 'Joint Reflection'. The fine old hymns Methodists and Anglicans share were sung, plus a special hymn, words and music by Molly Griggs and Pat Stapleton, adapted for the day. Items long familiar were in place to make us feel at home.

Frankly, with change looming, it has been a difficult summer; friends sharing their worries: *Somehow, I'm not comfortable there... I think I'll just go to the Sung Matins... Which Bible will we use?... What are you going to do?* Even: *Of course we should unite - I just hoped it would be after my time.* Think positive.

God is working his purpose out....
God is working....
God is.

AN EASTER SEPULCHRE IN THE NORTH TRANSEPT?

Photo Steve Humphries

An empty tomb reserved for Our Lord - or a common grave? It has been claimed that something as important as an Easter Sepulchre must be in a chancel, not a side chapel or transept.

There is certain record that vigil was kept beside an Easter grave - so there was a sepulchre somewhere! And when the floor was lowered, no grave was found beneath. Verdict - unproven - but if you visit on Good Friday you will find vigil still kept here.

NOT FORGOTTEN

Palmarsh, on the West edge of Hythe, regards itself as a community in its own right (and not to be confused with West Hythe, a different place again!) It was, indeed, once completely rural and separate from the main town. In-filling with housing estates and a small shopping centre have linked the two along the East-West coastal route, the A259.

Nevertheless, Palmarsh can boast its own Church and Community Hall, a state Primary School, a Public House called the *Prince of Wales* and, within living memory, a Post Office. It also has - or had - Nickoll's Quarry, from which large quantities of gravel were excavated from the early 1960's onwards, leaving pits which have been turned into a watersports centre for sailing and water-skiing, and fishing. But the Quarry is now sold for a major housing development; the increase in population - and the number of cars - is likely to impact severely on the whole area. How many of these new residents will find Holy Cross? It is there for them.

The Parish of St Leonard comprises THREE churches: St Leonard's itself, St Michael's (formerly in the Tin Tabernacle and now in the former Methodist Church with a new modern name, the Methodist Anglican Church Centre), and Holy Cross in Jubilee Close, just off the A259, a small mission church built in 1958.

In nearly thirty years of writing about this town, I have never, to my shame, written on Holy Cross, though every other church in Hythe of every denomination has had a feature: usually an anniversary was the occasion for some research and an article in the Parish Review or the Civic Society Newsletter. For some reason, the fortieth anniversary of Holy Cross Church in 2008 passed unnoticed and unregarded by me, though the small dedicated congregation celebrated it heartily at the time. Consequently I began this article, written specially for this book, to make up for past omissions.

I started (as one does nowadays) with Google. There, on Holy Cross's own website, is the very article ready written! It is by Anne Tolputt who cites her sources as gleaned from material collected by the late Mrs Jessie Lynch, from Flora Laundon's sermon preached on the Anniversary, and from various friends and members of the church. She charmingly adds: *'If any of the information is incomplete or incorrect, I ask the reader's forgiveness'.*

It would not be honourable to cut and paste from that perfect history. It tells you everything you need: who designed Holy Cross, who built it, who named it, what it cost, and by what means and through whose generosity it was equipped and furnished.

A nice touch is that Canon Newman, then the Vicar, felt that the builders should have a place of honour at the Service of Dedication, so the workmen all donned their Sunday best and sat in the front two rows. Incidentally, Tony Clarke, an Assistant Lay Minister, who still worships and conducts services there and reports on its activities in the Parish Review, was one of those builders. Anne Tolputt, too, still pays regular visits though she has moved to Hawkinge. And Sister Christine Morris has long been a tower of strength. I said they were dedicated.

This Parish was once deemed a 'teaching parish' and so had a Curate 'learning his trade'. Holy Cross was the ideal training ground where he or she would have a degree of independence, yet the support of the mother Church. Those days are long gone in the Church of England, where many a vicar now has seven or eight churches and may well have to whizz round two or three of them every Sunday.

A LEGACY OF LOVE
– AND SELF-INTEREST

A recent appeal for legacies omitted an important fact: a study in 2001 showed that a charitable bequest may be good not only for the recipient but for the donor also, for those who write such a Will live at least another thirteen years.

These are the statistics: men who die without having made a Will die, on average, at sixty-nine. Men who do make a Will die at seventy-nine. Men who make a Will containing a charitable bequest die at eighty-two. (For women, add two years to all figures).

It has to be admitted that, unfortunately, the average interval between writing your Will and dying is only 4.2 years. Presumably, if you make a new Will every 4.1 years, you will live forever - but then St Leonard's would never get your money!

WHERE ARE WE?

We are in The Soldiers' Chapel, the North Transept, St Edmund's Chapel, Hythe's Saxon Church - they are all in the same place, of course, the area on your left when you stand at the foot of the Chancel steps facing the altar. We are in the space I find the most interesting, historically, in the entire Church.

The early 13th Century Chancel, as completed by the Victorians in the 1870's, is grander, with its three storeys, its columns and carvings, its Gothic roof, its glass, its fine sedilia and piscina. But historians tell us the North Transept was created almost certainly out of the remains of a *Saxon* chapel when the Norman church was widened in the early 12th Century, and the style of that high narrow arch on the West wall does suggest it belongs to an earlier period of building. The floor here was not levelled down to match the rest of the church until the 1870's restoration - good evidence that use was being made of an earlier building.

Hythe's earlier church was dedicated to St Edmund and he is the centre figure in the large triple window on the North wall. But oddly, though this window is clearly conceived and surely executed as one design, its parts commemorate different dates: St Augustine, on the left (with a roundel showing him making his pitch to Ethelbert and Bertha at Ebbsfleet in 597), has a dedication date of 1858. St Dunstan, Archbishop, is on the right, with a date of 1932. And St Edmund in the centre panel is dedicated to a child of eleven (pictured, kneeling), with a dedication dated 1929.

I do not see how these three separate images and the three families seventy years apart, who presumably paid for them, got together to create one balanced whole. The answer must lie buried in the Vestry Minutes. Incidentally, this window survived the German bomb and doodlebug; whereas the windows up in the Chancel were shattered, and the pieces had to be picked up and arranged in a plain glass setting after the War. But the great East window was too much destroyed even for that, and had to be completely renewed to a modern design, controversial in the 1950's, though I think no longer so.

That still leaves the name *Soldiers' Chapel* to be explained. We know that when the School of Musketry was founded in 1853, the Army Commandant negotiated with the Vicar for space for his students' Church Parades. The Parish Council was initially reluctant (think of a Vicar today turning down a regular additional attendance seventy strong!) but, following Victorian principles of class segregation, they finally accepted the soldiers *in the Transept*! To keep them at a distance, a new entrance was created for them by opening up the Saxon doorway which had been bricked up for the previous several hundred years.

There is an even simpler explanation for calling this transept the Soldiers' Chapel: on the walls around are concentrated many military and family memorials. Every one tells a story of loss and grief and pride: in the 19th Century the big killer in foreign parts was Enteric Fever. The Indian Mutiny ('Killed by a mutinous sepoy...') accounted for more. Then the Killed in Action in the Boer War and the Great War: so many young men, (Age twenty, Age twenty-one, Age nineteen...). The fine record of the Finnis family, a family tree of honour... The tablet to Lt Hart of the Madras Light Infantry on the East wall (aged twenty-five, another Mutiny victim), is curious: it is 'Erected by his bereaved and afflicted parents who deplore *the loss of a beloved son removed thus suddenly from them in the pride of life'*. The lettering is incised and the letters filled in in black on the pale cream stone, until the point italicised is reached when the remaining lettering is incised but left unfilled. Did the Vicar intervene? Was exception taken to that word 'deplore'? Who are we to question God?

Pause in sympathy at the window in the North Choir aisle, dedicated to Lyall Brandreth of the Royal Fusiliers, a former Instructor at the School of Musketry, Killed in Action in June 1915: his widow records, alongside his death, that of Lilias Joyce their 'little daughter and only child', who had died in January of the same year, soon after his departure for Gallipoli, one may guess.

Most poignant of all is the Hamilton Memorial brass (on your left as you climb the steps from Chapel to Choir aisle). Major Hamilton RA died in 1884 aged only forty-seven, a grievous loss no doubt to his widow, but he left a fine Victorian family of four sons and three daughters. The upper brass records the fate of the sons, three of whom died in South Africa: Ernest, age twenty-three, Killed in Action 13 May 1900; Kenneth, twenty-four, died of enteric just seventeen days later; and Alastair, twenty-eight, killed by lightning, in 1902. Finally Patrick, thirty, of the Royal Flying Corps died on Air Manoeuvres in 1912. Margaret, Mrs Hamilton, herself died in 1920, age seventy-three, and her daughters Ethel, Hilda and Gladys put up the lower brass for her. The family arms bear the motto: Faithful in Adversity! No 'deploring' Providence here.

Parish churches are historical records; if the Pitkin Guide, or equivalent, of every church in England were bound together, I think we would have an incomparable 'Story of England', recording war and the pity of war, but telling too of lives spent faithfully and peacefully in the service of man and God.

*The Norman arch in the South aisle.
(Organ in its previous position beyond the Armada Chest)*

A 19TH CENTURY BATTLE: CHURCH v ARMY

In 1729 Hythe's Member of Parliament, William Glanville, ensured his re-election with gifts to the Church: he had a new wooden entrance door installed (replaced with glass in 2015) and donated new stone steps and at least one gallery.

By the end of the century, there were galleries in both aisles and across the back (where the organ pipes are now). Two are just visible in the picture below. It does not reproduce well but it is, I think, the only depiction of the galleries in St Leonard's.

The galleries were needed, for the box pews installed at private expense in the 17th Century were permanently rented out to families; indeed, when you sold your house, your pew went with it, so servants, those of no local address, and charity children, had to be fitted in elsewhere, usually on plain benches as befitted their lower status. In 1783, pews were installed at the West end (ie. as far away as you could get!) *for the accommodation of maid servants'.*

There were soldiers in Hythe too. In 1826 the Garrison Commander was asking for space for them, but *'the decided opinion of the parishioners* [was] *that there could not be found sufficient room to accommodate them without much inconvenience to the congregation'.* (In other words, *'It's Tommy this and Tommy that, and Tommy stay outside....').*

The General was not to be put off, and appealed directly to Lord Palmerston, then Lord Warden of the Cinque Ports. He, with unusual tact, wrote persuasively to the Vicar. The Parish Council relented and admitted '*70 men to each of the Services on the Lord's Day*'. Then in 1853, when the School of Musketry was established in Hythe, still more space was needed for the weekly Church Parade when the soldier students and their instructors marched behind a Band along Military Road, up Church Hill, and clattered into St Leonard's.

They were allocated the North Transept which is often still called the Soldiers' Chapel, and where are remembered on the plaques round the walls many of their comrades lost to mutinous sepoys, enteric fever, cannon ball or lightning strike. So many young lives, many of them trained at the School of Musketry here, lost in the service of Empire.

Church Parade, School of Musketry, Hythe

It is surely no coincidence that the door on the West wall - bricked up for five hundred years - was now unblocked (and the Saxon Arch uncovered), thereby providing a separate way in for the Church Parade and so maintaining an appropriate social distance from the residents (and those maids).

AT WAR WITH SALTWOOD

We have actual documented evidence that in the 13th Century St Leonard's Church had '*a certain Cross with holy Relics enclosed in it*'.

Traditionally it has been supposed the relics related to St Leonard himself. If so, they may have been there from the first, from the time around 1080 very soon after the Conquest, when a Norman Church replaced the Saxon, and the new Church may even have been named for this 6th Century Norman Saint because a bit of him was on offer.

A relic was a valuable possession, for it encouraged both the congregation in general and also passing pilgrims (of whom there were many en route from the mainland via Hythe Harbour to St Thomas Becket's shrine) to give generously, for everyone knew, of course, that every prayer said in the very presence of a Saint, every candle lit, would ascend to God more speedily and receive quicker and surer attention.

The relic (we do not know what it was – a bone, a hank of hair?) was a legacy, and left to Hythe on condition (stated, we are told, in the donor's Will) that the income it generated '*should in no wise come into the hands of the Rector...but instead should be disposed of by the men of the Village as they thought fit*'. By this was meant the Rector of Saltwood (for Hythe's Church at that time was a daughter church to Saltwood), and the Village meant Hythe.

Given his position of authority, the aforesaid Rector was distinctly unhappy with this financial arrangement, and in 1252 he complained to the Pope that the citizens of Hythe were doing exactly what

36

the Will said: spending the cash *'according to their wishes and as lavishly as possible'*. Hythe's imposing Church was visible to the pilgrims from the harbour, and the first Church they passed, so it had become the natural place for them to pause to thank God for their safe crossing of the Channel, *and to drop a groat or two into the collection box.* The Relic was an added bonus and the Rector's Church of St Peter and St Paul tucked away over the hill was left at a disadvantage. Not surprisingly, he wanted to exercise his right of control, and claim a share.

It must have been particularly galling to him to see the recently completed Chancel, a direct imitation of the Cathedral's in its design, magnificence, and the quality of its carvings and fitments, and the 'fair vault' below, possibly already furnished with charnel and inviting further donations. It was the last straw: it was all too obvious that the 'men of the Village' were spending the easy income to raise the status of St Leonard's as a shrine in its own right, even as Becket's Tomb in Canterbury Cathedral had been glorified in the years since his murder in 1170.

One wonders why Robert Anketil, a mere village Rector barely two years in post (quite long enough for the grievance to fester), chose to write direct to the Pope and not to his Archbishop (his neighbour actually, for Saltwood Castle was a residence used by the Archbishop). Perhaps he felt the latter's predecessor had taken too close an interest in St Leonard's and had facilitated the works? (An article speculating on these lines appears on page 103). Whatever the background and local politics, the

Pope ordered the Archbishop to investigate the Rector's complaint.

Sadly, the outcome of the dispute is not known. It would not have been beyond a Pope's powers to overturn a long-standing Will but perhaps that was not necessary. Respect for authority may have caused the spenders in Hythe to give way to the mother-church in Saltwood; the relic would not have been moved from its own church, but an arrangement to share the income could have been made.

Is it significant that Saltwood Church's Tower and North Nave were suddenly added around this time? And if, through sharing, Hythe's income were reduced, does this explain why work stopped suddenly when the chancel roof, the clerestory and the North triforium were yet unfinished? The completion of St Leonard's to its present glory had to wait another six hundred years.

The Barracks and Town of Hythe in 1829   [W.H. Ireland: "History of Kent"]

REMEMBRANCE IN HYTHE

Remembrance Sunday is taken very seriously in Hythe, a former garrison town which has close associations with the military and where troops still train on the Firing Ranges nearby. Remembrance Services in London and across the land engage even the people who 'don't do God', a time when we remember the losses rather than the triumphs of two World Wars, and many conflicts since.

The picture below will remind you of the stained glass window in St Leonard's, though there are variations. It is 'The Great Sacrifice' by James Clark (1858-1943). This is the original version, reproduced in colour in *This England* Magazine in Autumn 1994 which featured the work and the artist. The Editor gave us permission to reproduce it.

39

Originally called 'Duty', Clark's painting appeared in *The Graphic* in 1914, a presciently early date, for the wholesale slaughter had barely begun, though it was already clear the boys would not be 'home by Christmas'. It was an instant success. Copies were printed for homes and hospitals and especially for churches where it was often hung to form a shrine alongside the local Roll of Honour. The original was bought by Queen Mary and it still hangs in the Church at Whippingham near Osborne House. After the War, bereaved families could choose it from the Stained Glass Window catalogues in memory of their fallen sons, so it could be seen in several churches across the land.

There are differences of detail between the original and ours, but the characteristics which made it a popular choice remain: a handsome young man, mortally wounded, but cleanly, in a mentionable place, touches the very nail in the foot of our Lord. The Cross (much bolder in our version) stands on the British side of No Man's Land, and the mud and blood of the battlefield are suitably distanced. Clark was an artist better known for his depictions of decorous Victorian scenes; here he was uniquely inspired by the mood of the moment.

The Clark Window in St Leonard's remembers Robert Hildyard who was killed on the Somme aged nineteen. His body still lies alongside the serried rows of his comrades beneath a War Grave Commission headstone. Touchingly, in a glass frame below our Window, is the original crudely painted wooden Cross which first marked his grave. The article in *This England* mentioned two churches where similar windows were installed. I wrote to both of them, hoping to compare details. Now for the bad news: one letter was returned 'Address inaccessible. The church is demolished'. The second was answered by the Vicar of the Parish with the information that all the glass was removed from that church in 1993 when it was converted to 'affordable housing'. He suggested I write to the Diocesan Property Officer who kindly sent me photographs of the windows which had been removed - but no trace of the Clark.

I am all in favour of 'affordable housing' but churches are closing all the time and history is being lost: surely, when families buy a memorial, they have reasonable expectation that their fallen sons will be remembered for more than eighty years - as they certainly are in Hythe.

Hythe's Canal Bank Memorial originally listed one hundred and fifty-four names of servicemen killed in World War I, and sixty-one in World War II. A few others, accidentally omitted, have been added since.

To honour those who lost their lives in *later* conflicts, an additional ceremony has been added to the events of Remembrance Sunday in Hythe: a wreath is placed on the Memorial Angel which stands in the Council Chamber. This is the original Angel from the War Memorial. It was stolen (and the Memorial vandalised) in 1994 and unexpectedly rescued seven years later from the Canal. The Angel on the Memorial now is a replica.

Rev'd Desmond Sampson is Chaplain of the Royal British Legion (Hythe and Saltwood Branch) and also of the Hythe Branch of the Royal Air Force Association. His sermons at their ceremonies always contain a reminder that we can best give thanks by *appreciating* what those we remember fought for. They obeyed the call to arms, they did their duty, but they did not *give* their lives. Their lives were taken from them by the misfortunes of war:

Tranquil they lie, their knightly virtue proved,
Their memory hallowed in the land they loved.

View from the North
Note the unusual pointed mystery tower

A WAR-TIME MEMORY

St Leonard's Church was damaged twice during the War and the windows at the East end were destroyed. The photograph, though not of very good quality, shows the temporary replacement which remained in place until 1951. Because of wartime restrictions, linoleum was used to cover the gap!

QUESTIONS OF ARCHITECTURE

I came across this item in a Report in The Journal of Kent History (Issue 76, March 2013): it summarises a Study Day which took place in the Church of All Saints, Lydd.

One unusual feature is a double piscina allowing separate draining of the (Communion) chalice and water, thereby preventing wine and water mixing down the same drain. The Victorians installed this so that hands and chalice could be washed separately after it was established that transubstantiation did take place.

What a load of rubbish - and in a respectable Journal!

However, it did give me an excuse to revisit Lydd after an interval of some years. When I worked on the Ranges there, I used to attend services in All Saints from time to time. It was dull on the day I revisited but the Church (open and unattended) looked bright and inviting, the Easter flowers still in place and many signs of Parish activity. I went straight to the piscina in the South Chapel; this corner was the only part of the East end of All Saints to survive the devastating bombing in 1940. The rebuild undertaken in the 1950's was wonderfully done: monuments and walls restored, the East window redesigned, the chancel roof replaced in cream and gold - altogether a triumph of Faith and Fund-raising for a small town.

There is indeed a double piscina - two fluted bowls set into the wall with a trefoiled stone arch and it is most certainly NOT Victorian; it is plainly early 13th Century, as is ours in St Leonard's Sanctuary, which also has two bowls.

What were they for, and why are doubles rare? A basic piscina (we have two in St Leonard's) is a stone bowl, usually, as ours, inside a recess with a carved stone frame round the opening and sited on the South side of the altar; it was originally intended that the Priest about to celebrate Mass should wash his hands here, saying (from Psalm 26) *'I will wash my hands in innocency, O Lord, and so will I go to Thine altar'*. After the consecrated wine was consumed, the water used to rinse the chalice was poured into it to drain away *on consecrated ground*.

Early in the 13th Century, the very time our Chancel was re-built in its present form, Pope Innocent decreed the two actions were to be performed in separate bowls, so for a time, *twin* sinks were installed, greatly to the benefit of our Church, where the 'suite' of piscina and sedilia (seating for the priests) in finely carved stone was designed as one and fits perfectly into the space down the South wall of the Sanctuary.

In the 14th Century a later Pope changed the ruling, as Popes can do. (*'My predecessor was right to say so, by the same right I decree otherwise....'*) and decreed the rinsings were to be drunk by the celebrant - so a single bowl sufficed. Doubles are, consequently, rare, and precisely indicate the period of their construction.

Now we come to 'Transubstantiation' mentioned in that ignorant article: you may be surprised to read Transubstantiation (the conversion of the consecrated wine into blood) is now 'established'. When, pray? I suppose when Issue 76 of the Journal of Kent History appeared? Quite a scoop for that modest publication after two thousand years of theological dispute!

It is very meet and right to conduct a debate on the subject of Transubstantiation in a Parish Review, but I am hardly a person qualified to conduct it. Probably most C of E readers would concur with analytical chemists: that the wine is a *symbol* of Christ's blood, a very powerful symbol, the very foundation of the mystery of Communion, but chemically unchanged as we drink it. Today, piscinas are no longer used - they are often filled with flowers, and the rinsings are still consumed by the priest.

Before leaving the Sanctuary in St Leonard's, we may notice the unusual double sedilia: two seats side by side and carved in stone to match the piscina 'en suite'.

In a small church with a single priest, one stone chair was enough. In larger churches, a triple was the norm, each raised above the next, for Priest, Deacon and Sub Deacon. The congregation down in the body of the church on the public side of the Chancel Screen in those early times had no seating at all, of course, and the weakest, if unable to stand through the long services *'went to the wall'* - the stone benches down the walls and round the columns.

THE PORCH AND PARVISE

The Porch of St Leonard's Church was added to the South front in the 14th Century. Access to the room above was by an outside staircase; this room served originally, we are told, as a priest's dwelling and was called a Parvise - the word is related to paradise, but not in material comforts, for there is no evidence of water, sanitation or heating. It did, however, have a low round window to enable a man (on his knees) to see and hear the services in the nave below.

The new Porch projected across the Processional Path round the Church, so two doorways were provided to permit the Sunday circumambulation by congregation and clergy, priest and monks (perhaps bearing the Holy Relic of St Leonard) plus a choir of men and boys. The new Porch rendered inutile the three mass dials which indicated, like mini-sundials, the time of the next Mass, for they were no longer in sunshine. They are still there, to the right of the entrance door. (Did you know there is another mass dial (on its side) visible from the roadway, placed by a thrifty but dyslexic mason near the top of the perimeter wall just below the South-East corner of the South Transept?)

From the 1540's, the Parvise became the Meeting Room of Hythe's Mayor, Jurats and Bailiffs. It may have been a suggestion of theirs in 1722 that a new staircase to replace the old one, now presumably four hundred years old, would make a worthy gift to the town. Sir Samuel Lennard, Bart, one of the two Members of Parliament for our little rotten Borough (which had all of sixteen or so eligible voters), duly coughed up. In 1729, the Porch below was given a make-over by another generous MP, William Glanville, who replaced the main door into the nave, and provided the stone entrance steps.

The wooden 1722 stairway was taken down in 1825, and re-built in stone by Hythe Corporation. It is not clear why the Corporation paid for this work, since it was by then meeting in the new Town Hall on the High Street (opened in 1794). In fact, it continued to lay claim to the room, stored records there, and charged the Church an annual rent of one shilling until it became obvious that more expensive repairs were needed, and it seemed prudent to off-load it.

You cannot climb those steps now to visit the Parish Clerk without commiserating with her (or him) that such a lovely office sited high above Hythe as it is, has no view at all, since the windows are opaque. Despite their appropriate Gothic and leaded lights, they date only from 1863. Before that, as the Rev'd Dr Herbert Dale acidly comments in his History of the Church (published 1931), *'The upper part* [of the parvise] *had been disfigured by the intrusion of two common sash windows'*.

You see these in the photograph which shows a gentleman with a top hat (he must have stood very still for a long time. Was he the vicar?); entrance steps much narrower than now; iron railings and gates at the bottom (they would not long survive modern passing traffic); a decorative overhead lamp (compare the awful modern streetlight); a low squat roof, and two very out-of-place windows.

We do not know what preceded these sash windows - they look early 19th Century and may have coincided with the 1825 stairway, but that is guesswork. Really, the Porch at that time presented a mean and inappropriate elevation to the Norman nave behind. Fortunately the Rev'd Tatton Brockman of Beachborough Park stepped forward to pay for an excellent refurbishment.

In 1863, the Parvise roof was raised, with fine rafters inside and carved sandstone corbels outside. The double lancet window in a gothic stone frame

49

was installed, with another window on the West side, and a colourful stained glass picture of St Leonard himself (Patron Saint of Prisoners), visiting a prison cell, in the Porch below. This work was carried out just before amazing changes were made to the Soldiers' Chapel, the roof and the Chancel.

Truly, the second half of the 19th Century was for St Leonard's an astonishing period of building work, when funding matched faith.

Early 19th Century: Box pews. Plain East window, monopod pulpit. No clerestory or stone roof in the chancel yet.

THE CHURCH'S FORMER REREDOS

This photograph of the Altar was taken in the early 1930's and obviously before the German bomb destroyed the East window. It shows the sculpture of the Deposition of Christ from the Cross in its original place, as a Reredos. Carved from a single block of Carrara marble, the panel was the gift, in 1880, of the Curate, the Rev'd Claude Brown, in memory of his late wife; he must have been a wealthy man, for he had it designed by GE Street, ARA, and sculpted by HH Armstead, RA, at a cost of eight hundred pounds - a large sum indeed, at that time. Armstead also created sculptures for the Palace of Westminster and the Albert Memorial, and executed a large number of public statues and funerary works.

With his contribution, with Street's, and with that of JL Pearson, RA (who created our Chancel roof in stone), there is no doubt that in the 1875 Restoration, St Leonard's Church was served by the top men of the day.

This close-up photograph shows the detail of the Reredos; it was originally inside a wide carved frame in darker-toned alabaster. Pieces of this are still to be seen laid out in the Crypt.

The scene shows the preparation of Christ's body for the tomb after His Crucifixion. He appears as a rather older man than we might expect; the Virgin Mary, Mary Magdalene and, presumably, Mary Salome, are depicted offering tender care. The curtains are held back on each side by Pre-Raphaelite-style Angels, creating a theatrical framework, much of its period.

As our Church Guide says, 'Its deep swirling lines give it an almost sultry appearance'.

The bearded man on the left is 'the rich disciple', 'good and righteous' Joseph of Arimathea, the 'honourable counsellor' (he was a member of the Jewish Sanhedrin) who features in all four Passion narratives: he had gone boldly to Pilate to request he be given care of Jesus' body and offered his own tomb, still new and unused, to receive it.

Despite this boldness, interestingly he is stated by John (19.38) to have hidden his discipleship for fear of the Jews.

We might have expected Nicodemus to be depicted, since he too is reported as sharing the task of ritual preparation with Joseph. But the placing of the figures, the focus on Jesus as the figures lean tenderly over Him, and the overall design, leave no space for another person.

The different details, presented in the various Gospels about Joseph of Arimathea, bring him to life as an historical figure. Elsewhere, in Apocryphal writings, he is said to have cared for the Mother of Jesus in her later life (as did John, of course). But in medieval times, his name became linked with the Arthurian cycle as the keeper of the Holy Grail. It was claimed that he travelled to Britain and became the patron of Glastonbury. With or without such accretions, Joseph is certainly a fascinating man.

In 1938 the Reredos was moved, with its frame, to its present position against the wall of the South Choir Aisle because the Vicar said (according to the Vestry Minutes) *'that the doctrine teaching is incorrect'*.

There was certainly debate in the Church of England at that period on where the Vicar should stand when administering Communion - whether at

53

the end of the Altar, facing the congregation or facing East in the older High Church position.

So was the Reredos in the way? Or was the carving itself, with the Three Marys (a Roman Catholic concept), out of tune with his and his Congregation's feelings? We may wonder how moving it to a different location only slightly less prominent would correct its doctrine.

In 1957 the alabaster border was removed (it is laid out in the Crypt now), leaving just the central tableau. Perhaps someone remembers this happening, and why?

At least we can still be thankful that this fine and reverent artwork remains and, I think, better placed than originally, in that the altar is less cluttered in its setting.

A GREEN MAN OR A
GALLIC GESTURE?

Church historians tell us that parts of the walls of Hythe's Saxon Church still stand, incorporated into the present walls of the North Transept. Evidence for that is in the Saxon arch (tall, and narrow-framed) in the West wall and, equally telling, in the fact that the floor level of an earlier building (three feet higher than the present floor) was retained when St Leonard's was enlarged early in the 12th Century. But when you look at the other side of that Saxon arch (now inside the Choir Vestry), you see what is obviously a later, Norman-style, arch (wide, broad-framed and elaborately decorated); how come a Saxon building acquired a Norman entrance?

Here, the historians must speculate. They came up with a convincing explanation: the Mayor, Jurats and Bailiffs of Hythe were used to holding meetings in the Church so, when they had a new Church to worship in, it was logical to retain the old one as a Meeting House and to give it a prestigious new entrance.

These were solemn men of standing, who would process up here gravely two and two of an afternoon, deliberating town matters (and perhaps pass on a little local gossip too, for they were human, and not above discussing the price of a sheep, the marriage of a Lord, or the taking of a thief). We may suppose that even as the new church walls rose alongside, the Jurats were raising a subscription list and engaging a Master Mason, getting a price from him for necessary works inside their meeting place and provision of an imposing doorway in the new style.

They would not have had to go far to find a Mason's yard, for England, following the Conquest, was in the grip of building fever - everywhere, churches, abbeys, castles and cathedrals were springing up. The much favoured Caen stone (a nice earner for the Normans) was being imported through the South coast ports (including Hythe) and hauled inland along the rough trackways by bullock cart.

The defeated Brits were paying for all this, of course, but perhaps not too unwillingly. There was a new optimism abroad after the fears of 'the end of the world' at the turn of the first Millennium proved unfounded. English apprentices were benefiting as they were being trained by the Norman masters in the art of stone carving and new techniques of building. [Our Jurats' problem was more likely to have been one of 'finding a builder' against local competition - it would be interesting research to list just how much building, both state and ecclesiastical, was going on within a short distance of here during these very years.]

Arches like ours were manufactured in the workshop and assembled on site; the carver had much freedom as to the decoration he favoured, and there was no slavish requirement to match one window with the next, or even one side of an arch with the other - the machine-made regularity we favour was simply not looked for. The pattern of chevrons round the arch is typical of the Norman fashion, and the capitals of the columns have a variety of plants and motifs, giving wonderful interest and richness, (and colour too, for the stone was often opulently painted), after the heavy plain solidity of Saxon work.

This individualism has given to our arch a fascinating extra feature: high up inside it, on the left side against the door, the unknown mason has carved - a human face. Is this our Green Man?

We all know the Green Man in tales of Faerie and as a jolly figure on a pub sign, but in a church his sprouting foliate head may be a symbol of Spring (birth, fertility and growth), or (more sinisterly) of Autumn, approaching winter, or a demon figure, one of Satan's tormentors, a warning to sinners.

He may appear as a gargoyle, a waterspout, a fountain, a misericord, a capital on a column, even a door knocker. But of all the photos I have seen of him, this face is unusual, one of very few, in sticking his tongue out. Make no mistake, this is not the usual foliage emerging from his mouth - it is a rude gesture!

I do wonder if our Mason (a Frenchman, after all) is casting a cynical and disrespectful eye on the self-important procession of the local high and mighty in their robes and badges of office as they pass through his doorway, and making his own sly comment on the venery, the rutting and strutting, the wheeling and dealing, the expense accounts, second homes and tax evasions of the ruling class?

INS AND OUTS OF THE EAGLE

A couple visiting St Leonard's commented on how clean and cared-for were the shiny red tiles and bright brass lectern - a tribute to the volunteers! Then the man suddenly asked - why is it always an eagle which is used for a reading stand?

In part, the thinking was that the eagle soars highest and sees furthest, and was therefore closest to the heavens and could even see God from afar. The strong wings of the King of Birds take it on high and distant flights, so the medieval churchmen who introduced it (in brass or carved in wood) into their churches, replacing previous simple reading desks in stone or wood, were using it to symbolise the carrying of the Gospel to the four corners of the earth. That's the answer our visitors got, and they went away satisfied. But there is more to it than that.

In Christian art, each of the four beasts which surround the throne of God and are described in the Vision (Revelation 4.7) represents one of the writers of the Gospels: Matthew is represented by the winged man, Mark by the winged lion, Luke by the winged ox, and John the Evangelist by the eagle. *Evangel* means the Gospel, the Christian revelation, so it makes sense to associate John with spreading the Word by readings from the Bible.

The church lectern used to stand in the chancel of churches, behind the screen. It was a dramatic move to bring it forward into the nave, and to read from it the Word in English. The pre-war photograph shows our eagle lectern in its place - what a lot its brass eye has seen!

That is the old East window in the background,

destroyed in 1940 by a bomb. Not everyone likes the Wallace Wood replacement but it does have a drama and concentrated power lacking in the bitty and muddled Victorian one. The marble Reredos below is a wonderful piece but it is too high. It makes the Altar cluttered, and it covers some interesting 13th Century carving. It was moved into the South choir aisle in 1936. Though less prominent now than it deserves to be, I think few will regret its removal there.

The previous organ is visible through the arch behind the bird: our historian Vicar Herbert Dale disliked it there, recognizing that it blocked the perfect perspective up the South aisle through the

Norman arch and on to the Lady Chapel. *'The pipes should be in the Triforium as at Canterbury,'* he says sadly, *'but this excellent arrangement would be costly'*. Then in 1936, that is exactly what we got, with the gift of the present organ, its pipes divided between the West end of the Nave and the 'blind storey' on the North side of the Chancel.

The photograph shows four *coronas* - hoops (of iron usually) - bearing a number of candles (twelve, even twenty) round the rim, and having a rope and pulley to lower them to be lit. We know there were lots of these circles throughout St Leonard's, but they do not appear on an 1887 print.

An illustration in Dale's History, though very close in time to this one, shows four white glass globes attached to each one, with an on/off chain below each - presumably there was a pilot light, and the verger walked round with a hook on a pole to turn on the gas. There is no sign of these in this picture, which is puzzling. Were they in the process of being converted?

If only we could ask the eagle – he'd know, he watched it happen.

PS. I confess this article was originally titled 'Birds of Pray'. Oh dear.

SCIENCE AND THE BONES

'This skull had a tongue in it, and could sing once…it might be the pate of a politician…- one that would circumvent God, might it not?' Hamlet V- Sc i

Sorry for the bitter quote - politicians rather attract them at present. [This article was written at the time of the revelations about Parliamentary expenses.]

The good news story is that the combined efforts of the Stewards raised the sum of seven thousand pounds in the 2014 season. The Bones have been a nice little earner, possibly even from the time in the early 13th Century when pilgrims came in on their pious way up from Hythe Harbour to Becket's Tomb in Canterbury. And not only an earner, but also a resource of great interest to scientists.

There were several theories on the origins of the bone pile, but modern thinking has ruled out a 'Battle with the Danes': with so many older people, so many children and women represented, it is perfectly clear these are not the remains of young men killed in battle. Also no longer believed, is that they are Plague victims - these were rapidly disposed of in pits of lime. Experts now agree the bones were lifted from the churchyard when the foundations for the Chancel were dug out. The critical bones (skulls and femurs) were retained, with the remainder cast into a Charnel House outside, where they quickly decayed.

All of us who have acted as Crypt Stewards have whiled away a quiet hour looking at that white-covered file on the bench in which is recorded the research carried out by the anthropologists, Doctors

Stoessiger and Morant in 1932. They calculated the Cephalic Index of a large number of the skulls (this is a figure computed by measuring from nape to nose and ear to ear) and discovered an anomaly: that they were not typical of modern England's population.

Since this Index could be an indicator of racial origins, they theorised that the skulls show descent from the Roman soldiers, the marines, merchants and mercenaries stationed or living in this area or using this Port during the near four hundred years of the Roman occupation, and that this influence (this gene pool we would call it today) continued into the Middle Ages.

The Doctors did one more thing: they measured the skulls of the Hythe children in St Leonard's School (not the Army children, for they were outsiders). The children queued up apprehensively while the people from London with their white coats, clipboards and callipers measured their heads. The conclusion reached was that the 1930's population of Hythe conformed to the English average: the unusual characteristics had died out.

Eighty years on, modern anthropologists consider this a crude study, though pioneering in its day. They now have more sophisticated research tools at their disposal, but craniometry is still used and, in conjunction with DNA, is still an indicator of racial origin. Moreover, scientific research has provided fascinating new details of medieval diet and illnesses which can now be diagnosed from tell-tale signs in the bone.

'Curiosities of Natural History' by Francis T Buckland MA, published in 1872, is one of the most interesting early studies of the bones, not for its 'science' (which is non-existent) but for what it tells us about Francis T Buckland! He was briefed on his visit that here were the remains of a battle with a Danish Army in AD 843 when prodigious slaughter was done: thirty thousand dead, left to rot on the beach, and finally removed into Hythe Church! [Since the bone house was not built until around AD 1200, it seems odd that no one in four hundred years mentioned this pile on the foreshore!]

Buckland sets out to distinguish whose bones they were. '*The distinction between them is marked*,' he tells us. '*The Britons are noble looking fellows*,' their skulls have a cavity '*which must have contained a large and intellectual brain... Their jaws are powerful but by no means brutish*'. The expressions show '*courage, stern determination, firmness...a fitter specimen of a well-formed human skull I never beheld*'.

But, oh dear, the Danes! '*Their heads are of a different shape...they are long and narrow...small, eyes diminutive, and rather sunk into the head, and the jaws project downwards and forwards as we see in many savages of the present day... Their hair is red and fox-like*' - still a Danish characteristic. You have to give Buckland full marks for his patriotism, and you might take a fair guess at his views on the Brussels' Treaty.

I wanted to know more about this bigoted man. I Googled him and discovered he was a doctor, a surgeon, with a love of dissecting and a pioneer of zoöphagy: his favourite research was eating his way through the animal kingdom, eg. mice in batter, squirrel pie, horse's tongue and ostrich. His guests sampled Japanese sea slug, kangaroo, guan, curassow (no, I don't know either) and Honduras turkey.

Buckland's home was famous for its menagerie and its varied menus. Here is his lively description of an adventure with a sturgeon:

The fish measured nine feet in length. I wanted to make a cast of the fellow... I was determined to get him into the kitchen somehow; so, tying a rope to his tail, I let him slide down the stone stairs by his own weight. He started all right, but... I could hold the rope no more, and away he went sliding headlong down the stairs... he smashed the door open... and slid right into the kitchen... till at last he brought himself to an anchor under the kitchen table. This sudden and unexpected appearance of the armour-clad sea monster, bursting open the door... instantly created a sensation. The cook screamed, the housemaid fainted, the cat jumped on the dresser, the dog retreated behind the copper and barked, the monkeys went mad with fright, and the sedate parrot has never spoken a word since.

His kitchen sounds fun (one wonders if the animals were menus in waiting), and I have revised my opinion of Dr Buckland, though our Danish friends are less enthusiastic.

THE UNANSWERED RIDDLE

Yet another article on the Bones and Crypt in St Leonard's Church! My thinking developed as I read through the work of past historians, but I have not resolved the riddle: was the Crypt built as an ambulatory for processions with the Saint's Relic, or as a repository for bones? Or both?

During the 13th Century, for reasons of medieval theology, many churches acquired a Charnel Chapel to house large quantities of skeletal remains.

The positioning and design of these chapels were remarkably similar: often semi-subterranean, often (as ours) a 'basement' to the existing church, with access from outside, and windows to permit daylight worship within. Here ordinary people (as opposed to those wealthy families who could found private chantries) could be remembered and prayed for in an atmosphere calculated to make the living reflect on mortality.

Our Norman Church (begun c1080) was extended twice as Hythe grew and prospered: in the 12th Century - when the nave, side-aisles and transepts were created, together with an aisled Chancel extending twenty-eight feet (on the flat) - and then again, in the 13th Century, by about twenty feet (when the floor level of the whole Chancel was raised in imitation of Canterbury Cathedral and the side Chapels, Sanctuary and Undercroft were added). This second extension was a surprising addition, fewer than a hundred years after the previous work; it has been suggested it was driven by a rich and now-forgotten donor.

The internal work certainly made this important Church on the pilgrims' route from Hythe Harbour to Becket's Tomb even more impressive, but perhaps the main motive was to create for Hythe a prestigious and fashionable Charnel Chapel?

Anne Petrie calculates no more than thirty-six graves might have been disturbed by this second extension, so the bones to put into it must have come from elsewhere: it was not unusual to import charnel deliberately, even from outside the Parish, to 'furnish' a new chapel, and more remains would be found gradually as graves across the churchyard were re-cycled. Very probably, remains were moved up to St Leonard's and added to the pile in later times when other churchyards in Hythe were sold off for building.

At the time of the Reformation, the doctrine of purgatory was discarded, chantries for the dead ceased, and Charnel Houses must have been dismantled or put to other uses - the one at Holy Trinity Rothwell was bricked up and discovered only by chance in 1700. And at the Reformation also, Saints' Relics were discredited and Holy Day Processions ceased. Our Crypt must have remained locked and unvisited until it attracted antiquarian interest in the 18th Century. Perhaps there are many more similar chapels awaiting discovery?

The problem with the 'bonepile' is that it *narrows* the Crypt, making it much less suitable to serve as a corridor for Holy Day Processions. Yet it has a door at both ends, which would not have been needed in a Charnel House.

In old drawings, the bones and skulls are shown spilling across the floor. So how did a chanting crowd of church officials, followed by the entire congregation, squeeze past?

The late Jack Barker quotes from this Report by Mr Codd, who worked with JL Pearson on the re-roofing of the Chancel in 1879:

It is extremely unlikely that the Crypt was designed to serve as a processional path... The archways...are inconveniently and unnecessarily narrow... The vaulting curves over, considerably reducing the available height...altogether insufficient for the passage of 'an army with banners'... The two doors are unnecessary: archways with iron grilles would be the obvious treatment. The procession would have been unsightly because of the different levels and singing [ie. chanting of Psalms] *very difficult. The highly ornate doorway on the South side indicates that the procession would have gone **in** there - the wrong* way. The old and infirm would have had great difficulty. Why go to that extreme cost for something which could have been done differently?*

Yet the stonework at the North entrance is completely plain, and the South so decorated that Leland, who valued the Church's estate for Henry VIII, commented on it (*'a faire old door of stone'*) when he visited in the mid-16th Century. Sadly, he does not mention any bones inside the *'faire vault'* - if they were there, perhaps they were so common a sight in the churches he visited as not to need to be mentioned?

Mr Codd has applied imagination to his knowledge of medieval church architecture and practice, and makes a good contrarian case.

If you seek certainty, you will be disappointed: there is much to discover in St Leonard's Church, secrets locked in its stones and bones. In the future, science may date and analyse the bones and teeth, and comparative research into charnel chapels may reveal more about the theology which lies behind them and how they were used. And perhaps an overlooked Will, or Diary, or Court or Vestry Record will turn up, and all will be made clear.

* The 'right' way is, of course, clockwise, as the sun appears to move - so *in* at the North door, *out* at the South. (Only witches move 'widdershins' round their cauldron).

The West Tower (before the Choir Vestry was built)

ANOTHER CONUNDRUM

This print shows the untidy state of the Crypt in past times. It was not until the mid-19th Century that shelves were built; before that, with skulls and bones spilled across the floor, there would have been little room for those regular medieval processions which probably included the whole congregation as well as the church hierarchy.

Yet expert opinion argues that the reason for building this 'corridor' when the Chancel was extended in the 13th Century was to provide a route round the Church to carry the Holy Relic *on consecrated ground*, and that the bones came from the graves in the South-East corner of the churchyard.

There are reckoned to be thighbones and skulls from around two thousand people in the Crypt; it cannot be that anything like that number were buried in that small area of the churchyard.

Graves were re-cycled in those sensible times and the removal of the odd bone when digging a new grave was normal: witness Hamlet, who watches the sexton turn up a skull as he digs Ophelia's grave, and asks, 'Whose was it?' The answer is 'Yorick's'.

69

If Hamlet is around twenty-five years old in the play and can just remember Yorick carrying him aloft, some twenty years must have elapsed - a reasonable time for a grave to be left before being re-used.

After that time little would remain, for coffins were not used, (nor grave markers for ordinary folk).

Every parish church had its 'charnel house' for any displaced bones and there they quickly rotted away.

It was still usual to re-cycle older plots in *Victorian* times. Artist Henry Bowler exhibited the picture below in 1855.

The mourner stares down into the newly dug hole, sees the disturbed bones alongside and asks, 'Can these dry bones live?' An affirmative hopeful answer is given by the fresh leaves, the word Resurgam ('I shall rise again') on the headstone, and the bright butterfly on the skull. But even as it was painted, Darwin was at work on 'The Origin of Species' and soon this touching faith was questioned as never before.

Presumably the bones displaced in our churchyard waited in the open for perhaps two years or more during the building of the Chancel and on completion of the work, the thigh bones and skulls must then have been stacked inside. The remaining bones of lesser importance were probably placed in a charnel house to rot. It must initially have been a very small pile inside the Crypt - there surely cannot have been more than twenty or thirty graves in the site of a mere twenty foot extension, so there would have been plenty of room for the Processions at first. But bones would have been added later, not as was once thought from battles, still less from victims of Plague, but from later re-cycled graves, and possibly from other Hythe churchyards in following years as these were disposed of.

Once the Processions ceased at the Reformation, there was no need for a corridor; the steps outside the North door were no longer used and were allowed to fill up with soil from above, the very doorway at the North end was forgotten, we are told, and the bone-pile within could fill half the width of the vault - as in the picture - as it does now.

I believe that the elevated Chancel in St Leonard's Church was created only in part to provide a processional route on consecrated ground - that could have been easily and far more cheaply accommodated outside, at the East end of the building.

Another reason, equally important, must have been to *dramatise* the Chancel and Altar - it is uniquely impressive for a Parish church - in order to mirror the design of Canterbury Cathedral: this was the first English church the Pilgrims en route from the mainland Continent would enter.

It was proudly visible from Hythe Harbour, it lay on their route to Becket's tomb, and it had additional importance in containing the relic (whatever it was) of a Norman Saint (to the chagrin of Saltwood, which wanted a share of the income that a relic generated!).

St Leonard's Church was just over the hill from the Archbishop's country residence, Saltwood Castle, and the Archbishop, probably Stephen Langton at the time of the extension, was boasting (true to character) to Johnnie Frenchman the skill of the English at church-building, and providing the Pilgrims with 'an antechamber to the Canterbury Experience'.

THOUGHTS ON BONES

If, indeed, as we are told, the bones buried in the South-East corner of St Leonard's churchyard were disinterred to clear space for the foundations of the new Chancel extension in the early 13th Century, they must have been temporarily stored, perhaps for two years or more, until the new building was finished - probably they were simply left in a pile, covered or in the open. There could not have been many, as I have argued previously [see page 67].

When the time came to put them in the new vault, only the skulls and thigh bones were moved inside. We must assume the remaining bones were simply placed in the 'charnel house' - a simple open-sided shed such as all churchyards needed at a time when graves were routinely re-cycled - to rot away. Why were skulls and thigh bones selected for permanent storage?

This image is used across the world to signify death or danger and it represents the whole skeleton. The skull, of course, is an obvious choice to retain, for it is the brain-case and still looks human; the brain is the person: his/her intelligence, personality, his/her *soul*. The significance of the thigh bones is less obvious.

Firstly, they are tough and lasting, so more likely to endure. But they are also near the sex. They represent a person's place in the sequence of the generations; they stand in general terms for the family of man and, in particular, for the actual individual family. They are a suitable metaphor for an age which had no concept of genes, so if you can't keep everything to represent your past, at least keep these. And, appropriately, it is from these bones that the 'ashes' are prepared, to be delivered back to the family after a cremation.

Two recent well-publicised examples show what modern science can do to investigate human remains. Everyone has surely heard of the certain identification by DNA of the body of Richard III found under a car park in Leicester; further bone analysis has shown not just his deformed physique and death wounds, but also how his intake of alcohol and rich foods increased from around the date he became king! He became a bottle-a-day man, drank much beer (safer than the water, no doubt) and feasted on swan, crane and heron.

Particularly helpful to scientists are teeth: they are formed in life, and so record our diet. Teeth have helped tell the story of a medieval princess.

The tomb in Magdeburg Cathedral (pictured during excavation), which bears her name, is 16th Century, so the chances that it actually contained the remains of Princess Eadgyth (think Edith) who died in 946 were considered slight.

Nevertheless, inside was a lead coffin also showing her name: it contained a female skeleton wrapped in silk and aged between thirty and forty.

But was it Eadgyth? Tiny samples of tooth enamel were taken; strontium and oxygen isotopes mineralise in the teeth as they form, so researchers worked out the levels of strontium present and compared them to the age of the rocks in different regions. It emerged that this lady had spent the first fourteen years of her life in the chalk regions of southern Britain.

Dr Alistair Pike, senior lecturer at the University of Bristol, explained: 'By micro sampling, using a laser, we can reconstruct the sequence of a person's whereabouts, month by month up to the age of fourteen.'

Isotope results exactly matched historical records of Eadgyth's childhood and adolescence in Wessex. Even a period of her life spent in a Winchester Convent showed up. She was the daughter of Edward the Elder, King of Wessex, so a granddaughter of Alfred the Great from whom descends our present royal family. At the rather late age, for those times, of twenty, she was given in marriage to Otto (later King Otto I 'the Great' of Germany) by her step-brother King Athelstan - a political alliance, of course.

One story tells that she and her younger sister Adiva were both presented to Otto, who was invited to pick which one he liked best: Eadgyth's looks and charm won out over her sister's youth. She bore him two children and he was deeply upset at her death. He went on to become Holy Roman Emperor, the first of the line of Ottos which ruled Germany until 1254 (just about when our Chancel was finished). After the indignities of her examination, the English Princess has been replaced in her German Tomb, her identity and life-history confirmed.

The on-going study of our Crypt bones by the St Leonard's Osteological Research Group tells us much about the health and diet of ordinary people in the Middle Ages. What more might be discovered? Our Liaison Representative with the Group, Mike Pearson, comments: 'Our aim is to have some of the teeth in the Crypt subjected to isotope analysis - for this to happen we need a friendly University with the appropriate equipment, formal Diocesan approval to allow the teeth to be taken away and, of course, FINANCE, as the analysis is a costly process.'

A RE-THINK ON THE CRYPT

I have previously posed the question 'Was our Crypt built as an Ambulatory or a Charnel House?' I can't find out who *first* suggested it was built as a 'corridor' so that our Saint's Relic could be processed round the Church on Holy Days '*without taking it off consecrated ground*'. That theory has long been an unquestioned article of faith, and especially so with our chief and most influential historians, the late Jack Barker and the Rev'd GM Livett; the latter, in 1912, made the most meticulous measurements we have of the Church and imaginatively described the circumambulation. (Published in Arch Cant XXX).

The first Norman Nave and Apse were built around 1080 *alongside* Hythe's previous Saxon Chapel, and stretched from the present Tower to the line of the present Chancel Arch. A major extension (1120+) incorporated the Chapel, added a matching though slightly smaller South Transept, and introduced side aisles with rounded arches, a Screen and a Chancel with side chapels; it extended (according to Livett's drawings - presumably based on archaeological evidence) to a line slightly short of the present Sanctuary steps, with the same floor level as the Nave, (though the Saxon area remained a metre or so higher).

With building possible only in the summer season, this construction must have taken several years. Now comes the extraordinary fact: barely fifty or sixty years from the completion of that expensive work, which itself must have created a magnificent and worthy building, a further extension in 'Early

English' style took place: the Chancel floor was raised over a basement 'crypt', the Sanctuary and side chapels, the arcade, windows and columns were created with a South triforium, and buttresses were built outside to support the added weight on the unstable hillside.

Arches throughout (with an exception in the South aisle) became fashionably 'gothic' in shape. The most expensive stone was used for the column clusters in the arcade. The carving was of the highest quality, rivalling that of Canterbury Cathedral. Why ever was this done? A modern historian suggests, without evidence, that it was the pet prestige project of a rich and forceful donor; (if so, he ran out of money, for the ceiling and clerestory and North triforium were not completed for another five hundred years). I prefer to think it was designed with magnificence to awe the pilgrims en route to Becket's Tomb (see page 72). Whatever the reason, did the additional twenty feet in length, right to the East churchyard boundary, create a problem for Processions with the Relic?

If the basement crypt was intended to provide a route for those Processions, it is singularly ill-designed, being too narrow and too low (see page 67). In any case, why should not a Relic leave consecrated ground? Readers of 'Don Camillo' will remember processions through his little town; today, in Bruges, as just one example, the relic of the Holy Blood is kept in its Basilica throughout the year, but paraded through the streets on Ascension Day. Anne Petrie (who has helped my research from her Catholic perspective) found the following in

'Portable Christianity: Relics in the Medieval West (c700-1200)' by Julia MH Smith:

Reliquaries were intended to be moved around. They were integral to the performative aspect of medieval Christianity, for they would be brought out and placed on or hung above the altar on special feast days, carried in ritual processions from one altar to another inside the church, and moved outside into the open air for a wide variety of purposes. Monks and clerics sometimes carried relics far and wide to raise revenue; to take them to the tenants on church estates; to face down warring factions and pressurise them into suing for peace in the presence of the holy; to bring healing to the sick; to seek intercession at times of famine or epidemic.

I like that word 'performative': this was drama - the new Church was built for the performance of the Mass, a stunning and awesome ritual which took place deep in the Chancel beyond the screen. John Betjeman writes: 'There was an attempt in these Early English abbeys and churches to create a semblance of Heaven on earth, with their stone, colour, music and ritual'.

Now go outside and consider the South wall of St Leonard's and the 'terrace' over the family vaults; before this was built, the South (and judging from its decoration, the main) entrance to the Crypt was via a staircase from the road (as described by Viscount Torrington in 1790 – see page 84).

Similarly, before the South Porch was added in the 14th Century, entrance into the Church through the South door must have been via a flight of steps from the roadway. In other words (and I have not seen this pointed out before) if the processions, moving clockwise, came through the crypt, they must have descended one set of steps, moved along the road, and re-entered the church up another set of steps! And if they could do that, they could perfectly well (and more coherently) have avoided the crypt and processed down the sloping road at the East end of the new extension rather than awkwardly dividing the participants by taking the entire congregation through a low and narrow corridor.

But if not for Processions, why was this expensive basement added on to St Leonard's Church? At the very time of the work, Charnel Chapels were being built in many locations - *at least sixty have been identified so far.*

Here human skeletal remains could be kept permanently above ground in large quantities. The chapels are mainly semi-subterranean, not fully underground, accessed from the exterior of the church building, and constructed so that their South and/or East walls are directly in line with the South and/or East wall foundations of the church building above, permitting openings or windows to be made so worshippers could visit, pray, and view the contents, and a permanent Charnel Chapel Priest might take confession here.

Does this sound like our crypt? It would explain the sheer quantity of skulls and bones amassed inside - far more than disturbed or re-cycled graves could produce - for it was normal to import charnel from elsewhere to furnish a new chapel.

In short, on the architectural and historical evidence, we must revise our Guide Books. A Charnel Chapel was the fashionable must-have accessory to a prestigious church in a wealthy town in the 13th Century, especially one with a sense of importance as a Cinque Port on the pilgrim route to Canterbury. And a Charnel Chapel is what we have.

Before the Luftwaffe provided St Leonard's with a car park

AN EXTERIOR VIEW

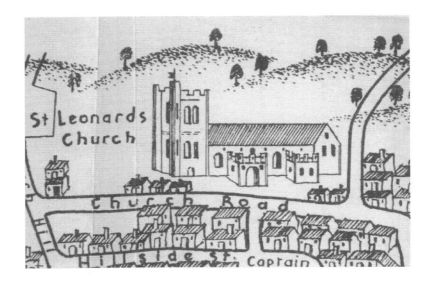

This picture of St Leonard's is taken from the 1684 'Hythe Hospital Map', drawn by Thomas Hill, who was obviously having a bad day. It really is nothing like the church we know! It is understandable the South Transept and the Tower look different, for Hill was drawing before they were rebuilt in 1750/51. (The Tower he shows collapsed in 1739 - a dramatic event, for it is recorded a party of visitors was about to climb it 'for a view', but they were delayed waiting for the key. It tumbled down even as they stood around chatting in the nave!)

But Hill shows no priest's room over the porch (certainly in place in the 14th Century); there is no sign of the 13th Century chancel, its roof higher than the nave roof then and now; and where are the West door and the distinctive three East windows, all obvious on many other early views? Hill did get 'Church Road' right - it is not his fault that the name was changed to Oak Walk in the 19th Century.

HYTHE CHURCH.

The other thing he got right were those houses on the North side of the road. We know this from the picture above - a rare drawing, by someone called Dudley: a lady is standing in the doorway of her home which was built where the oaks and the high retaining wall opposite the Vicarage are now. She is chatting to passers-by.

The Church in the background clearly shows the re-built Tower, the top of the priest's room, a crenellated South Transept (compare Hill's), and, beyond, the high roof of the Chancel and clerestory windows. Really, it is a detailed and informative drawing. It can be dated between 1750, when St Leonard's got its new Tower, and 1863, when the priest's room was re-roofed; the costumes perhaps suggest the late 18th Century? If you look at that high wall where these cottages stood, there are (or is this my imagination?) signs in the stones of filled-in features, doors or windows, but quite low down, as if the road level is higher today.

The curious thing is that there are graves in the churchyard above, where the cottages stood; they look very old, and the dates are obliterated. They must have been dug after the demolition of the cottages, when the ground level was raised.

The houses Hill shows at the other end of the Church also fit the evidence we have from other sources. The Crypt floor level was lower than now, and GM Livett tells us, in his Architectural History of the Church, that the Holy-day Processions came through the corridor and paused at a 'Station' on the South side: *'an area once occupied in part by cottages and now by [Family] Vaults'*. Afterwards, the processions must have moved up steps to the side door in the Porch.

Viscount Torrington visited Hythe in 1790 and describes ordering dinner at The Swan, finding the Sexton, and entering the Church and Crypt: *'It is a good edifice,'* he remarks patronisingly, *'with an attached dry above-ground Building in which are piled an immense quantity of human skulls'*. He goes on to describe his meal which seems to have been the cook's night off - tough meat and indifferent port.

Our Churchwardens often have great difficulty in obtaining a Faculty from the Diocese, even for simple works, like a new handrail in the Porch. I sympathise, but must wish a similar Faculty system had operated in past centuries: it would have made the job of the researcher so much easier. What would you give to visit St Leonard's when Hill or Dudley drew it?

St Michael's, 1930s

THE ALTAR-ATIONS OF HISTORY

This lithograph of St Leonard's Church by Robert Groom was published in 1860. You notice at once the insignificant altar and the dominant pulpit.

After the Restoration, the emphasis was less on the Sacraments at the Altar and more on the Sermon, and the design of church furniture reflected that. Indeed, St Michael's, with its central pulpit in the Methodist tradition of Wesleyan preaching, is another example of design following church practice.

The Pulpit is shown without the sounding board which once helped project the preacher's voice down the church. The board, recently refurbished, now hangs safely on the wall of the modern Choir Vestry after a hazardous life as a table.

The print shows the medieval 'temporary' ceiling, before the 1875-87 vault replaced it. The box pews were rented to families (an important source of income) and each has its little door to be opened for the worshippers by a 'Pew Opener' in return for a tip.

Obviously the pulpit had to be high for the preacher to be seen; the monopod design came into use even before the Reformation, though not all medieval churches had one - there were severe restrictions on preaching, not lifted until the reign of James I, so they were not needed.

An edict of 1603 stated there should be in every church *'a comely and decent pulpit to be seemly kept for the preaching of God's word'*. After the Civil War, the Sunday Service was conducted from the reading desk, and from the Altar only on infrequent 'Sacrament Sundays', so the Pulpit became the focus and was sometimes actually moved to the centre of the chancel opening, even obscuring the sanctuary. Some were provided with an hourglass, an idea which might be followed still! Many bore the inscription *Fides ex Auditu* (Faith comes through Hearing).

You have to wonder if the Deedes Memorial in our Church (still in place today and visible on the print) with its family motto *'Deeds not Words'* was a sly comment on the sermon; (that would somehow be typical of an ancestor of Bill Deedes!) Our present much lower pulpit went in with new pews in the 1875-87 refurbishment.

Meanwhile, the design of the Altar too was changing. In the early English Church, altars were usually of wood, but in 1076 Archbishop Lanfranc ordered they were to be of stone - a slab with Crosses at the corners and centre to represent the Five Wounds of Christ, placed on stone pillars, one of which could be hollowed out to contain Holy Relics. (Was our relic of St Leonard placed here?) There were minor altars, too, dedicated to saints of local importance and placed in side aisles or against the Chancel screen - see the still-visible colours in the stonework of the South pillars marking their locations.

Then, at the Reformation, relics and stone altars were ordered to be destroyed - the slabs were thriftily re-used as steps, hearth-backs, or gravestones. Edward VI firmly decreed wooden tables, but it was typical of the style of Elizabeth I that her later decree required them to be *set in the place where the altar* [formerly] *stood'* and added that those who still had a stone altar could retain it if they chose - she knew how to make use of the forces of tradition where no doctrinal point was involved.

The first altar rails were provided, not so much to kneel at as to keep dogs from fouling them! Gradually, the altar and its rails became fixtures against the East wall, but not for long. Came the Commonwealth, these 'monuments of superstition' were destroyed. Light tables with folding or pull-out leaves were made and placed in the nave, when required, for the communicants to sit round, as at a meal at home.

Traditional fixed altars and rails returned with the Restoration (much besides the Monarchy was 'restored' then) and Communion began to take the form we would recognise. But it was still an infrequent event: Victoria and Albert went but thrice a year; Victoria opposed Bertie's request that he might take the Sacrament every Sunday as some of his Equerries were now beginning to do.

With Communion so infrequent, it is not surprising that the altar at which it took place seemed of less importance in the weekly service than the Pulpit. In Groom's print, it is barely visible over the rails, and this must have been so until 1881 when the Rev'd Claude Brown placed above it, in memory of his wife, the lovely marble Reredos, representing the Deposition of Christ from the Cross which is now placed in the South Choir Aisle.

Wood or stone, fixed or portable, large or small - variants wrought by time and politics, by fashion and accident. Does God smile at our hysterical reaction to changes which do not matter?

A SAXON CHURCH IN HYTHE?

Jack Barker, our late respected Church Historian, put forward in his published papers and in his lectures the case for the Saxon origins of St Leonard's Church. There has to have been a Chapel in Hythe before the Conquest and here was the place for it, where the old Roman Road from Studfall to Dover crosses the main road from Hythe Harbour to Saltwood and Canterbury.

There was a piscina (still in place) and an apse at the East end, an Easter Sepulchre on the North wall, and an entrance at the West end. It was common practice to continue to use a traditional site for a new church.

Jack argues convincingly that the new church (begun around 1080 soon after the 1066 Invasion), and to be called after the Norman Saint, St Leonard, was built deliberately alongside the old chapel of St Edmund, (a Saxon Saint), to give continuity of worship for the Hythe congregation.

Initially then, the old and new buildings would have stood *separately*, side by side, and the old was appropriated by the Jurats - the councillors of the town - for their meetings. We speculate this was when the entrance doorway acquired its Norman arch (now inside the 1950's

Choir Vestry), perhaps to give dignity to the place thenceforth to be used for their deliberations.

This theory accounts for the unique 'back-to-back' Norman/Saxon stone doorway on the West wall of what we now call the North Transept. On the left (with Victorian steps) is the 'Jurats' Door' and, on page 90, the door inside the Saxon Chapel. The wooden door could not be made to fit both arches exactly.

When the two buildings were merged into one (c1120) this entrance was no longer required - it was bricked up and the inside plastered over. In the picture, we see the ground level of the steep churchyard has gradually covered the lower half of the arch and the steps. It was re-opened, the soil removed, and modern steps provided in the 1840's.

It is an extraordinary fact that from the 12th Century to the 19th, the floor level of the transept remained some three feet above the floor level of the rest of the church. The point where the levels changed must have required protection from accidents: a low wall perhaps? We have no illustration of this, but the evidence for the change of levels is still visible in the change in the type of stone used: below the arch, below the Easter sepulchre, and where the remains of the eastern apse are visible, Victorian sandstone has been inserted. It was also necessary, when the level was changed, to add steps *down* on the inside.

The only explanation for the different levels has to be that the builders made use of the chapel already in situ and in just the right position for conversion to a transept, which they were able to match to a South transept opposite.

The Tower between the two buildings has been compared to an Irish Round Tower. It has a very un-Norman beehive shape at the top and is much higher than would have been necessary for access to the roof level at that time.

The spiral stair inside the Tower gave access to the Rood Screen (via that little door above the pulpit), but not directly, since it ends at the wrong level and needs a little sideways projection. It leads also to the Triforium and Clerestory floors and finally to the roof leads. But here, also, is an oddity, for despite their experience in building spirals, this one ends facing the wrong way and a plank bridge has had to be installed at the top.

At the base, too, it gave our builders some problems for it is thicker and wider than it need be, has an unaccountable irregular footprint, and is not concentric as a spiral normally is. They had to cut a corner off the North wall to give sufficient width to the aisle to permit processions into the chancel. It spoils the symmetry of the North aisle arch and, really, it gets in the way, standing here as it does. It is surely not the way you would build it if you were starting from scratch. We are left with the strong impression they had to fudge and bodge to make things fit, making use of what was there.

It has been argued this Tower makes more sense if it were once free-standing (a pre-1066 watchtower, perhaps against Norman raiders?) or even that it may have been attached to the Saxon chapel. However, there is no denying it has been keyed into the walls of the chancel and its entrance door is appropriate to the level of the main church.

So debate continues, but the fact of the Saxon origins of our church is generally accepted.

A PARISH TREASURE

The new Parish Secretary was busy in her office 'sorting out' and 'tidying up', as new brooms do, when she came across a velvet-lined wooden box containing a bible; she placed it in the deep window embrasure in the Parvise to show off its nicely carved and varnished surface. I spotted it there and admired it but what I didn't realise, until I took a closer look, is that the leather bound book inside, with wooden boards carved to match the box, is not your standard Authorised Version, but a GENEVA Bible, and the spine bears the date 1614.

Still more interesting is that it is a 'Breeches Bible' - so called because we read at Genesis 3.7 that Adam and Eve *'sewed fig leaves together and made themselves breeches'*.

A marginal note helpfully explains these are *'things to gird about them to hide their privities'*. The Authorised Version has the couple in 'aprons' which has always seemed to me an overly domestic image; 'loincloth' might be the ideal translation, but that word had not appeared. The New International and Good News Bibles both use *'coverings'* which is rather unimaginative.

So, the Parish has a 'Breeches Bible' - where did it come from? At one time it was in the possession of a family called Keen who recorded their details on the reverse of the New Testament title page: Edmd Keen born 1691, Sara Keen born 1734, Robt Ware, and other names and dates, all crudely written as by hands unused to holding a pen. The front fly leaf is signed 'Henry Pritchard 1886' in an educated hand, and he has added 'Bound 1887 in wood panels': the initials 'HP' are carved on the back panel. Clearly, it was he who had this done (greatly devaluing the book of course), and he had the box made to hold it.

What was the link with Hythe? The Hythe Research Group has recently discovered that Henry Pritchard was the Vicar of New Romney from 1899 until his death in 1933. He was ordained deacon in 1886 and priest in 1887, so it looks as though it was an ordination present to him, perhaps from his parents. But we can only speculate on why it should have come to Hythe rather that New Romney. Miss Laundon used it in her 'Time to Celebrate' display, but that was in 1999 and since then it has been forgotten. Rev'd Norman Woods remembers only that it was there when he arrived (than which the memory of man goes no further!) and has no knowledge of its provenance.

What is the importance of the Geneva Bible to history? An English translation was not new: Henry VIII had commissioned one and placed it in every church, but he hoped to keep the genie in the bottle by forbidding labourers, servants, and women (though he exempted noble women) to read the New Testament.

During Bloody Mary's reign, Protestant exiles gathered in republican Geneva and 'working day and night' they published a version there in 1560 of which nearly one third was not God's Word at all, but comment on it. And comment which King James was later to condemn as *'very partial, untrue, seditious, and savouring too much of dangerous and traitorous conceits'*. Indeed it threatened the finely balanced 'Elizabethan Settlement', that wonderful compromise which gave something to everyone: Protestant in doctrine, yet retaining Bishops, Vestments, Churches, the sign of the Cross at Baptism, and especially (from James's point of view) the Divinity of Kingship.

The exiles dedicated their Geneva Bible to Elizabeth, newly crowned on Mary's death. She accepted the honour cautiously for typically she *'wished to favour neither Papist nor Gospeller'*. It was instantly a popular success: it was so accessible. The translation was by William Whittingham (who was related by marriage to Calvin), and drew on several previous translations and, above all, on the unfinished work of the martyred master of prose William Tyndale.

It divided the text into verses (the first bible to do so), and gave simple summaries at the head of each chapter; the font was easy-to-read, and there were notes to explain the 'hard places', it had maps and pictures, *'two right profitable and fruitful concordances...on the sense and meaning of the Scriptures',* a page of *'certain questions and answers touching on the doctrine of Predestination'*, and the quarto edition was cheap enough for a tradesman's family to buy.

In the following years, its popularity grew. With this in the home, who needed a priest? Here was the rub, of course: the bishops especially hated the Geneva Bible because it undermined their authority and their traditional role of interpreting God's word to the people. In this they had the support of Elizabeth's successor who was determined to suppress it. Geneva was an independent Republic with a strong interest in spreading its political ideas - in a monarchical age the very name signalled revolt against the establishment.

The side notes and explanations to the text were revolutionary. But from its first arrival in England there was no stopping it, especially when the defeat of Spain's Armada proved God to be a Protestant and the Puritan extremists became more radicalised than ever. It went into more than one hundred and sixty editions: a population of six million, many of whom were illiterate, bought half a million copies. It had to be suppressed!

King James, uneasy in his new capital, hated it from the first as dangerous and traitorous, that is, literally, the work of traitors. He twisted Psalm 105 and 1 Chronicles 16.22: *'Touch not the Lord's anointed...'* (despite the sense of the whole passage) into a justification of the Divine Right of Kings, for was not he recently anointed at his Coronation? No, said the Protestant scholars: the passage refers to the people, the rank and file, for all Christians are anointed at baptism and therefore they must not be harassed even by royal authority. Ideas like this if unchecked would overthrow the entire structure of church and state. Yes, it had to be suppressed. The only way was to produce something better - and without those seditious notes!

In 1604, James set up his unpaid Committee of around fifty mainly Oxbridge scholars who were working in three locations, communicating in Latin without benefit of email and, in 1611, produced the work we know and love, Apocrypha included.

Know and love it we may today, but the simple fact is its arrival on the scene was greeted with polite disinterest. For many years it remained the bible of the establishment rather than the bible of the people. Scholars who had not been selected to work on it were the most vociferous critics, and Puritans were quick to say that Parliament should authorise a Bible, not a monarch - the lines of the forthcoming Civil War were already being marked out.

The title page of the St Leonard's Geneva Bible tells us it was 'imprinted at London in 1614 by Robert Barker, Printer to the King's Most Excellent Majestie, *cum privilegio*'. These two italicised words mean 'under licence': Robert's father Christopher had bought the privilege for himself and, by extension, for his son, and so had the monopoly of official printing. As the Geneva Bible was so popular and therefore profitable, he quickly ensured it would be printed in England - and by himself. This was permitted until 1616 when James caused printing of the Geneva Bible to cease in

98

England. But it could still be imported, and imported it still was until Charles I, advised by Archbishop Laud, argued that English printers needed protection and banned its importation.

At last sales of King James's Bible began slowly to grow, though Robert Barker did much less well out of the printing; production costs amounted to three thousand five hundred pounds, he needed partners with whom he quarrelled, he over-reached himself, had cash-flow difficulties, and died in a Debtors' Prison - though King's Printer to the end.

There were criticisms of the book's inclusion of the Apocrypha, of its apparent hostility to Puritanism - the dominant strand in political thought up to and during the period of the Commonwealth - and especially of its misprints, for Barker had saved money by cutting down on proof-readers and underpaying them. It did not help his finances either when he was heavily fined for rendering Ex 20:14 as *'Thou shalt commit adultery'*.

Then came the Restoration. With a King on the throne again, Protestantism was discredited as a system of politics and religion, and suddenly a Royal Bible was seen as holding together church and state, bishops and monarch. With its misprints corrected and growing familiarity, the literary and spiritual influence of the King James Bible from the 1700's to World War I has been incalculable; it has gone from strength to strength for its authority and dignity, especially in conservative Protestant America, whence (from Texas, actually) comes this judgement:

'If the English of the Saint James Bible was good enough for Jesus, it is good enough for me'.

AN ARCHITECTURAL HISTORY

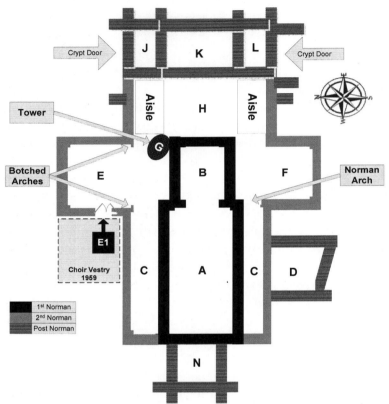

My thanks to Sean McNally for this scale Plan

A. Norman Nave c1080. Traces of its windows visible high in the N wall. Entrance at the W end (no Tower then). Named after a 5th Century Norman Saint (perhaps because a Relic was on offer?)

Hythe's redundant former **Saxon Church** of St Edmund **E** alongside was then appropriated by the town's Jurats for their meetings.

B. Norman Apse. No details of its size or design exist.

C. Nave Aisles added **c1120,** with round arches through the former side walls. Done not to increase capacity but rather to create space for processions, for drama and liturgy. Round arch into the S Transept remains. Awkward botched work needed to combine new church with old.

D. S Porch 14th Century. 'Parvise' above, probably accommodation for the Priest, later used as Town Meeting place for Jurats and restored 1863. Now the Parish Office.

E. N Transept, on footprint of the Saxon Chapel. S wall removed when buildings merged **c1120** but floor level (3' higher) left unchanged. Double-sided Arch **E1** bricked up but re-opened 1875 and floor level lowered. Later variously called Weller or Soldiers' Chapel.

F. S Transept c1120. Re-built 1750 by the Deedes family and contains their memorials. Built nearly to the edge of the Church boundary, so unusually, smaller than the N Transept.

G. The **Staircase Tower**, date debated. Gave access via doorway above the Pulpit to a Screen with undoubtedly the full-size figures of Christ on the Cross and Mary and John alongside; above this level gives access to N and S Triforium, Clerestory and Chancel roof.

H. The first **Chancel Extension c1120,** with side-aisles. Floor level with nave. It completed the 12th Century Church but we have no details of its appearance. If there were graves in the area built over, any disturbed bones must have been re-buried.

101

JKL. Extended Chancel c1220. Surprisingly soon after, came the final raised Chancel extension – a deliberate copy of features of Canterbury Cathedral with a Sanctuary elevated over an Ambulatory or Ossuary. We suppose it was at this time arches throughout the Church were re-built in Early English style; but the vaulted Chancel roof, the Clerestories and N Triforium were not completed, and a cheaper and lower wood and plaster ceiling was installed. Nevertheless, this Chancel must have impressed pilgrims en route from Hythe Harbour to Becket's Tomb; the marble and stone, the columns and carving, are expensive and finely carved. St Katherine's Chapel **J** may once have been a Vestry. The Calvary Chapel **L** was once the Lady Chapel. The 'temporary' ceilings (in position for six hundred years) were removed and the present vaults and N Clerestory and Triforium installed in 1870, surely in accordance with the medieval Master Builder's first intentions.

N. West Tower ?c1230. Collapsed 1739. Re-built 1749. W Door entrance. Spiral stair from Tower Vestry leads to Clock mechanism and Bell Ringers' chamber.

Choir Vestry/toilets/kitchen added in 1959 and re-furbished after the 2000 Millennium Appeal.

TOURIST TRAP
An Historical Fantasy

Archbishop Stephen drummed his fingers on the oak table in the Great Library and stared into the glowing logs in the deep fireplace. He liked staying in Saltwood Castle - he remembered it had also been Thomas Becket's favourite residence, his *manerium predilictum*.

He liked it all the more because King Henry had been forced to restore it to the Church in the aftermath of Becket's murder, when His Majesty did public penance on his knees for his share in that event.

It was in the Knights' Hall, just a few yards away outside, that the murderers had planned the deed with that most evil of men, Ranulf de Broc (some said without a candle between them, lest they saw the evil in each others' eyes).

That was an event, an assault on God's senior churchman in England, which shook Europe. But the workings of God are mysterious indeed, and there is no doubt, Stephen reflected, that things had turned out much better than might have been expected since that December night forty years ago. At least the Tomb was in place, and the Cathedral was getting richer every passing day with pilgrims' gifts.

It is true that relationships between Church and State had been through rough times since the late King's abasement, under Richard, and especially under John: he himself as Archbishop had been kept out of his Chair for eleven long years by King John, but he had put his name (the first to do so) to the

103

Magna Carta, a sweet moment, and full reinstatement had come at last with the accession of the boy-king Henry III. His aspirations had been thwarted for so long; now he would rule his See and build to God's glory.

In these more settled times, the pilgrims were coming to Becket's blessed tomb in growing numbers, but Canterbury, as a late starter, was not yet even near the top of the Visitor Tables; fortunately, a couple of miracles had been helpful in demonstrating the efficacy of a visit and a gift. But Stephen felt he must do more; he especially wanted to attract the foreign trade.

He had brought the problem down here to Saltwood, to think it through in the calm countryside, away from the bustle of Canterbury. He concentrated his mind now; start at the beginning: what did these foreign people want? There was the sea-crossing, uncomfortable and dangerous, nothing he could do about that. Then the landing at Hythe Stade, transfer from the ferry in a small boat, or even lifted over the shingle in a fisherman's arms.

Then it got better: the Church of St Leonard was in sight on the hill ahead and the road beyond to Canterbury (the very road the murderers had taken, he remembered grimly) was smooth and open, and above all, kept safe by the King's soldiers - even prices in the inns and lodgings en route were controlled. And, at the Cathedral, the machinery was in place to awe the visitor, to help him spend his money on tokens and the like, and to re-assure him his visit was godly. What more could be done?

Stephen Langton applied some lateral thought; he was a builder by nature - he was improving his

Cathedral, he was now spending on this Castle of Saltwood. It was hardly surprising that his thoughts turned back to St Leonard's Church in Hythe, the first English church the pilgrims saw, lying right on their route. That church had in fact been widened and extended not too many years before. It had the additional advantage of lodging a Relic of the Saint Himself, making every prayer said there, every candle lit there, doubly effective, as every Christian knew. People were bound to go in to give thanks for a safe sea voyage. Surely it made sense to provide a WOW factor here, to make it a foretaste, an *antechamber* to the Canterbury Experience? Then with a bit of luck they would go in again before the return crossing, and each time, of course, the Church would be richer by a few groats.

He hadn't visited Hythe recently, but remembered it well enough to think about what might be done. He called for paper and ink and new candles. He would prepare here and now on this table a rough plan for the French Masterbuilder, the one with the Yard at Dover where the stone could be brought in from the Caen quarries.

He knew the hillside was none too stable, but this was God's building, and He would protect it - still, no harm in an extra buttress on the South side. The stonework would be of the finest, with marble too, from Purbeck, brought by sea to Hythe Harbour. He would have to tear down the recently completed chancel and then he would build on to the nave the finest chancel of any church in England, not to say Europe. He knew exactly the effect he wanted - lightness and elegance.

105

He had not seen the new Cathedral at Salisbury which was building even now, but he had seen the plans: the graceful columns in clusters, the pointed lancet windows - at Hythe he would have three at the East end. It would be surely the only Parish Church chancel with three stories - a triforium gallery over the Arcade and a clerestory above that to light up the vaulted stone roof.

There would be aisles North and South for the choir and monks' processions, and a Lady Chapel. Above all, the floor level would be raised like the Canterbury Choir, with steps into the Chancel from the nave, and steps again up to the Sanctuary and High Altar. Below, there would be an arched vault fitted out as one of those Charnel Chapels now becoming so popular. And he'd send his own trained workmen down to do the wall paintings and new-style 'dog tooth' carving, with a piscina and sedilia, all en suite - he'd seen one done like that last year, near Cambridge.

The arches, especially the great chancel arch, would be in the new pointed style, of course, with Christ on the Rood screen, flanked by Mary and John, life sized. He remembered a sort of tower at the side there, that might be in the way - it would spoil the long vista from West to East through the delicate new side arches. Well, the tower could be removed.

He was enjoying this: no Dean and Chapter to interfere - a pet project of his own. And while they were about it, if the money lasted they would replace all the round arches down the nave in the new style.

106

That was the question: would the money run to all that? Hythe was a rich town with its fishing fleet, its market selling the produce of the rural hinterland, its role as a Cinque Port exporting wool and sheep, importing beers and wines, with the busy route to and from Normandy where many of the newly created 'English' barons still had estates. Yes, Hythe should be able over a few years to afford a building on this scale.

The foundation would be enriched with pilgrims' gifts. They might not be so pleased up in Saltwood at this ambush of the high-spenders, but you can't please everyone. And if his plan couldn't be executed all at once, they would work in stages: the clerestory could wait and a lower wood and plaster ceiling would serve until the next generation paid for stone. Even the triforium could wait, or they might be able to complete one side as a pattern...

The fire had turned to grey ash. He was still working, the table covered in sketches and plans, when the bell rang for lauds. He made his way slowly out to the Castle Chapel nearby, to be met in the chill dawn gloom by his chaplain hovering questioningly on the sward outside. Archbishop Stephen acknowledged him gravely and silently but gave nothing away prematurely. It had been a night well spent, he thought with satisfaction, a *constructive* night.

A DEBATE ON DATES

The article (see page 103) about St Leonard's as a 'Tourist Trap' (to lure in the pilgrims en route to Canterbury) was admittedly an 'historical fantasy' - no more than an imaginary reconstruction of what might have happened in Saltwood Castle one night early in the 13th Century: I suggested Archbishop Stephen Langton thought up the idea of enhancing the pilgrims' Canterbury Experience by extending and glorifying the Church's Chancel. Did this really happen, and just when?

Our historian, the late and much respected Jack Barker, says firmly it was *'in 1200'*, meaning *around* that date. He supports the idea (already proposed by others) that it was done to meet the expectations of the growing numbers of pilgrims en route through Hythe to the tomb of Thomas Becket, murdered in 1170.

It is hard to imagine a re-build on this scale proceeding without support and direction from Canterbury, especially as the Church was attached to the Manor of Saltwood which, in turn, had belonged to Christ Church Canterbury, and hence to the Archbishop, since the time of Canute.

But there may be more to say. In June 2011, a student, called Matthew Cooper, submitted to his Examiners his Dissertation (for which he got a Distinction) on THE ARCHITECTURE OF ST LEONARD'S CHURCH AND ITS CONTEXT for his MA in History of Art.

He shows that St Leonard's Church is an outstanding example of medieval ecclesiastical architecture, with some unique features. He dates the Chancel into the 1230's onwards, chiefly on stylistic evidence: the quality of the workmanship and the authority of its design and execution could hardly have been achieved at the very start of the 'Early English' period. Could it really have preceded Salisbury Cathedral (begun 1220, completed 1258), the exemplar of the new style? Or did St Leonard's actually lead the way in the style wars?

One factor Cooper does not mention, but which could be crucial evidence of an even later date than he proposes, is the *double*-bowl piscina in the Sanctuary. Lawrence Jones of the Historic Churches Preservation Trust writes: *'This type can broadly speaking be assigned to the reign of Edward I (1272-1307)'*. Before that period, *'one drain was provided for the lavabo* [ie. washing the priest's fingers] *and the ablutions* [ie. rinsing the chalice]. *After that date the ablutions have always been consumed by the priest'* [so back to one drain only].

If that is correct, our Chancel has to be dated towards the *end* of the 13th Century, which rules out Stephen Langton as the driving force: he died in 1228. He became the nominal Archbishop in 1207 but was forced to live abroad until 1213 because of the Pope's disagreement with King John. He was then suspended from office in 1215 for his support of the rebellious barons; he was not secure on his cathedra until 1218 when he had ten years left to live. Langton was a known builder, and he had big ideas: the debts incurred for his magnificent arrangements for the 'Feast of the Translation of St Thomas' in 1220 were a burden to his next four successors! But if he planned our Chancel, as I fancifully imagined (see page 103), it had to be in his last decade of life, so favouring Cooper's dating, especially as work could hardly have started immediately. You can Google the list of his successors - most last only a year or two until the middle of the century. If an Archbishop was indeed behind the work, it is difficult to nominate one with the continuity to see it through.

Cooper does not mention the influences of passing pilgrims or Langton's contribution, if any, or even the involvement of Canterbury. He suggests the possibility that this re-build of the Chancel, surprisingly soon after the extensive work in 1120 onwards, was due to a wealthy local benefactor, now unknown to us. There is no evidence for this suggestion.

What is unarguable is that the medieval design remained unfinished for hundreds of years; it was finally completed to the best guess of what the Master Mason had intended in the great refurbishment of the Church in 1875-87 (as recorded on the plaque on the South-East column) by Messrs Street and Pearson, and paid for by voluntary contributions raised by the 'loving care and zeal of the Vicar, Rev TG Hall, at a total cost of ten thousand pounds'.

This graceful print opposite, c1835, shows the 'temporary' plaster ceiling which lasted to the 19th Century! Hall's Fund paid for the removal of that ceiling and for the new stone vaulted roof here and over the side choir aisles, for the North side clerestory and triforium, the tiled floor, the pulpit, and the new timber roof over the Nave.

Original roof, no clerestories, no North triforium

Other 19th Century works were the lowering of the North transept floor and an East window of stained glass (which was destroyed by enemy action in 1943 and replaced with the present design in 1951).

How plain the Chancel shown in the print looks to our eyes, whose taste in church decoration was formed by the Victorians, and how insignificant was the altar - the emphasis then was less on the Sacraments than on the Word.

111

OUR VICTORIAN CHURCH

You have only to step over the threshold of St Leonard's to know you are in a church which was re-furbished in Victorian times: the colours and patterns in the floor tiles, so like those laid in thousands of suburban 19th Century houses, indicate that. Until these were laid, our floor consisted of plain grey slabs.

The walls, on the other hand, until the Reformation, were a riot of lurid colour, and told the Bible stories to an illiterate congregation. Capitals, mouldings, statues, the life-size tableau of Jesus, Mary and John on the Rood Screen in the Chancel arch, were bright with colour; the glowing stained glass cast over all a *'dim religious glow'* (in Pugin's approving words), and created an atmosphere of mystery and awe.

Henry VIII should not receive all the blame for sweeping away this glorious artwork: it was his young and fortunately short-lived son, Edward VI, a convinced Lutheran, who sent out the iconoclasts on their mission of destruction, so that Elizabeth, a reign later, inherited churches bare and stripped of their age-old finery. We have, in consequence, in Hythe, a grey building - grand and imposing certainly, but (apart from some glass) grey and austere. Yet Victorian taste was far from austere - it enjoyed fussy decorative details, it liked to provide objects galore to interest the eye.

Look at Folkestone's Parish Church, for example. *'Half a ruin'* when the Rev'd (later Canon) Woodward arrived there in 1851 from Hythe where he had been Curate; the re-building and decorating

112

of St Eanswythe's became his life's work, and how well he was supported by the gentry of the town who were happy to contribute to a scheme which so matched the taste they exhibited in their own homes.

Look at Holy Trinity, too, consecrated in 1868, a prime example of Victorian brick Gothic, paid for by the Earl of Radnor as part of his project to expand Folkestone westwards along the new *'Sandgate Road'*. Interesting that the Church came first, as part of the project: today, developers bribe Planning Committees with swimming pools, not churches, when they apply to expand the town. Interesting too, that so out-of-favour was Holy Trinity's style between the Wars that the decision had been taken to demolish it and centre the Parish on Christ Church, just down the road - until German bombers reversed the plan.

Back to St Leonard's. Do we regret the loss of colour? Our many visitors seem to find our Church grand, but above all, peaceful. This may be because it is not restless, not relentlessly obtruding its personality, but leaving it to the worshipper or viewer to fill in the emptiness for himself.

To illustrate that thought, I find those much praised swirly blue sea-pictures in the windows of Winchelsea Church a complete distraction - they make me sea-sick! How styles of worship change, and how furnishings and decorative fashions change with them; after the introduction of the English Prayer Book in 1549 the laity were encouraged to take part in services for the first time. Indeed, they understood the services for the first time!

The removal of the Chancel screens had brought priest and congregation into the same room.

Parliament abolished East Altars and rails, as Communion was taken at a wooden table set up in the choir or even in the Nave. Pulpits became *'three-deckers'* from which Priest and Clerk could conduct the entire service, and no need even to enter the Chancel; seating was introduced (benches first and later, box pews).

The Victorians hated the 'Prayer Book Churches' of the 17th and 18th Centuries. Few of them (around seventy, is one estimate) survived the ruthless restoration carried out under the influence of the High Church Movement emanating from Oxford in the 1840's, which re-introduced ancient (sometimes pseudo-) medieval rituals requiring vestments, deep chancels and *'proper'* more highly decorated altars with candles, often dignified with a Reredos; those dominant pulpits were replaced with smaller ones, and family bench-pews were installed and rented out. Pictures and prints of our Church over the years show all these changes have happened here.

Before becoming a novelist, the young Thomas Hardy trained as an architect. His work concentrated on church refurbishment; later in life he regretted what he had done. In 1881 he joined the recently-formed Society for the Protection of Ancient Buildings (still active today) which tried to prevent architects (and vicars) from *''spoiling' churches in their Tractarian zeal'*. He wrote that such buildings *'hold together memories, history, fellowship, fraternities'*. Hardy makes a vital point: if we are to keep our bearings, there has to be a thread of continuity - we can take only so much change.

We may regret the widespread 'vandalism' which occurred under the influence of the Camden Society, the Ecclesiologists, and the doctrines of Pugin. But St Leonard's is representative of a tradition of layout and furnishing we are comfortable with because - those seventy exceptions apart - it is the only form we normally ever see when we visit churches, and familiarity breeds content!

Moreover, in our case, we have a special reason to be thankful to the Victorian architects who worked here in the 1870's and '80's. Whatever they did to the floor and the pews, the pulpit and the altar, they also completed our Nave roof and Chancel in the form which its 13th Century creators intended.

TURBULENT PRIESTS

This final article is not about the church but about us, its 21st Century congregation. It was suggested by my happening to read of two quarrelsome priests and their absolute commitment to their interpretation of their faith, commitment, if need be, to the very death.

Divines possess a singular ability to be troublesome to authority; in the reigns of Queen Elizabeth I and King James, it would have been hard to predict the emergence of our Anglican Church, so noted, we like to think, for its moderation and tolerance, out of the extremes of Puritanism and Catholicism then in conflict.

Hugh Broughton (1549-1612) was a Hebrew scholar who had his first disagreement with the Archbishop of Canterbury while still in his twenties – over the interpretation of scripture. Unwise, you may consider, in one hoping for preferment! He must have realised this, for he exiled himself to Germany and continued his sniping from there for the rest of his life. He was not easy to put down on matters scriptural, for he could read the Old Testament in the original, and he had translated the New Testament into Hebrew from the Greek. He found fault with both the Bibles then in use in churches (the Bishops' Bible and the Geneva version) and demanded a new translation, immediately, before souls were lost through reading false doctrine.

As it happened, James was even then (1604) convening his Conference at Hampton Court with

116

no thought of authorising any such thing. He was perfectly content with the Geneva Bible but he wanted it without its subversive notes which dared to be critical of kings; his aim was to define his own position as King under God, and possessed of a Divine Right. The Puritan faction attended the Conference in sombre black; their agenda was to remove all traces of the old Catholic Church (including vestments, kneeling – and bishops). The Bishops attended in all the pomp and finery permitted them under the Sumptuary Laws. Despite their differences thus visually illustrated, when the proceedings closed, all factions departed at least partly pleased: they had talked themselves into creating the Authorised Version of 1611.

James appointed fifty-four scholars as translators – and Broughton was not among them! I have not discovered if his chagrin and fury at being thus snubbed contributed to his death in 1612, but certainly his fault-finding with the new translation was bitter and difficult to counter. He castigated Archbishop Bancroft as *'a deadly enemy to both Testaments...and an assistant to the unbelieving Jews'*. Only on his deathbed did he lament his bad humour and regret that he was too easily provoked.

My second troublesome priest is the arch-Puritan Stanley Gower (1600?-1660), a preacher of renown – and endurance: it is said that on fast days he entered the pulpit at eight or nine o'clock in the morning to pray and preach extempore until five o'clock *'if daylight continue so longe'*. Of course, he would not wear the surplice nor use the sign of the cross at baptism; he blamed the bishops, *'an anti-Christian institution'*, for the 'abuses' in the church

117

of his day, and denounced the Royalist clergy as the *'devill's orators'* (for he acted as spy, and reported on Royalist sermons preached in Hereford Cathedral). As Rector in Dorchester, Dorset, described as *'the most Puritan place in England'*, he even authorised himself to ordain clergymen – the role of a bishop.

Gower was at his most troublesome as a member of the Westminster Assembly of Divines, a Council of Theologians appointed by the 'Long Parliament' in 1643 to restructure the Church of England. The Long Parliament was Puritan in character, and opposed to the religious policies of King Charles I and William Laud, his Archbishop of Canterbury. These two supported the 'old rites' and reinstated worship practices such as vestments, kneeling at communion, bowing at the name of Christ, and the placement of communion tables at the East end of churches. This was rank papacy! Charles's High Anglicanism plus the fact that his wife was a Catholic made many of his subjects – and not just extreme Puritans – suspicious.

This dispute was to end in civil war, Charles's execution, and Laud's; and Gower was at the centre of affairs during that very time. We who tell ourselves we have progressed to a charitable acceptance of the opinions of others, and who make a virtue of being tolerant and inclusive, may give a superior 21st Century smile at the petty battles of these radicalised Christians. Arcane though their quarrels were, they were carried on by committed men who believed in something, believed enough even to die for it. How do we compare with that?

118

AN HISTORICAL CALENDAR

597   Arrival of St Augustine and his companions in Canterbury.

1026   King Cnut gifts Manor of Saltwood and Hythe with the Saxon Chapel of St Edmond to the Priory at Canterbury.

1066   Norman Conquest. Manor of Saltwood given to Christ Church Canterbury.

c1080   Norman Church of St L with Apse built alongside Saxon Chapel and separate from it.

1085   Doomsday Book (no mention of St L) – the 225 'burgesses of Hede' shown as belonging to Saltwood.

c1120   Hythe Market and Harbour prosperous: St L widened in Norman style, S Transept and Chancel added, Saxon Church incorporated as N Transept but with West doorway blocked and floor level unchanged.

1170   Becket's Martyrdom. Thereafter increasing numbers of pilgrims en route to Canterbury make offerings in St L.

1207   List of Vicars extant from this date.

1215   Magna Carta.

1220   Chancel extended in Early English style with Screen but with 'temporary' ceiling. Nave arcades replaced in Early English style. Floor level raised and 'Crypt' corridor created; displaced bones from churchyard lodged within?

1252   Dispute (outcome unknown) with Saltwood on ownership of profitable Relic(s) kept in St L.

1278 Charter of Edward I granted to Hythe.

1282 First recorded ordinations in St L.

1293 Hasted records French fleet offshore: two hundred French soldiers landed and are slain on the beach. Other raids recorded.

1348-90 Black Death in Hythe.

Early 14th Century Nave arches enlarged and re-shaped, roof raised. Porch Parvise Tower built.

1390-95 Fire in town – three hundred and sixty homes burnt, one thousand homeless (? unlikely totals).

1400 Loss at sea of five ships, one hundred men and boys.

1400 Pope Boniface grants indulgence to pilgrims who give alms to Saltwood Church and Hythe Chapel.

1412 Request to King to abandon Hythe, but instead a new Harbour built by common effort – essential to survival of town.

1413 First record of clock on Tower.

1480 Record of Peal of Bells, Organ, Choir of men and boys, Benedictine Monks.

1538 Act of Parliament: Parishes to keep Records of Marriages, Births and Deaths.

1534-59 Period of turmoil: serial changes to doctrinal position of the Church. Pilgrimage abolished; Becket's Tomb destroyed. In St L, destruction of altars, chancel screen, statues and decoration. Consequent loss of income.

1555-57 Under Queen Mary married incumbent deprived of living and three Hythe men martyred.

1560	Incumbent removed for refusing to accept Protestant rule.
1566	Earliest extant Church Registers begin, traditionally stored in 'Armada' Chest and now stored in the Canterbury Archives.
1575	Hythe granted Mayor and profitable Fair.
1580	Earth tremor shakes bells. Damage to Tower.
1588	Spanish Armada. Hythe provides – or pays for – one manned ship of fifty tons.
1649-60	Execution of Charles I. Restoration: Charles II.
1729	Galleries erected 'for the Charity Children'. New high pulpit with sounding board.
1739	Collapse of Tower, visitors escape.
1750-51	Deedes family re-build Tower and S Transept.
1780	Repairs to North Aisle (? post-quake damage).
1794	Hythe Town Hall built; henceforth Church rents Parvise from Town Council for five pence a year.
1816	New pulpit. Old sounding board removed to Vestry.
1819+	New pews replace box pews.
1841+	N Transept floor lowered at last and its West doorway unblocked.
1844	Independence from Saltwood.
1863	Porch and Parvise re-built; new windows and staircase.
1875-87	Street and Pearson restoration of Nave roof and Chancel vault; new choir stalls.
1875	Removal of galleries.
1880-81	Mosaics added to pulpit.

1893	Gift of Reredos Church of St Michael and All Angels opens in 'Tin Tabernacle'.
1901	Queen Victoria clock installed.
1936	New H&H Organ (extended 1991). Reredos removed to South aisle.
1940 & 1944	Bomb and Doodle Bug destroy Chancel windows, create car park.
1951	New East window by Wallace Wood.
1958	Holy Cross opens in Palmarsh.
1959	New Choir Vestry built on North side of St L.
1975	Calvary Chapel dedicated.
1993	Two bells added, making a full peal of ten.
2000	'Millennium Appeal' for Restoration raises two hundred and fifty thousand pounds.
2011	Congregations unite in St Michael's Methodist Anglican Church Centre. 'Tin Tab' sold.
2014	Porch and South doors glazed. Servery in North Aisle.